The Waltz of the Toreadors

A PLAY IN THREE ACTS

by Jean Anouilh

Translated
by Lucienne Hill

SAMUEL FRENCH, INC.
25 WEST 45TH STREET   NEW YORK 36
7623 SUNSET BOULEVARD   HOLLYWOOD 46
LONDON   *TORONTO*

THE WALTZ OF THE TOREADORS

Copyright, 1953, by Jean Anouilh and Lucienne Hill

Copyright, 1958, (Acting Edition) by
Jean Anouilh and Lucienne Hill

ALL RIGHTS RESERVED

CAUTION: Professionals and amateurs are hereby warned that this play, being fully protected under the copyright laws of the United States of America, the British Empire, including the Dominion of Canada, and all other countries of the Copyright Union, is subject to a royalty. All rights, including professional, amateur, motion pictures, recitation, public reading, radio broadcasting, television, and the rights of translation into foreign languages are strictly reserved. In its present form the play is dedicated to the reading public only.

Where the play is available for amateur production royalty will be quoted on application to Samuel French, Inc., at 25 West 45th Street, New York 36, N. Y., or at 7623 Sunset Boulevard, Hollywood 46, Calif., or to Samuel French (Canada), Ltd., 27 Grenville Street, Toronto 5, Ontario, Canada.

Stock royalty quoted on application to Samuel French, Inc.

For all other rights than those stipulated above, apply to Dr. Jan Van Loewen, Ltd., 81 Shaftesbury Avenue, London, W.1, England.

Copying from this book in whole or in part is strictly forbidden by law, and the right of performance is not transferable.

Whenever the play is produced the following notice must appear on all programs, printing and advertising for the play: "Produced by special arrangement with Samuel French, Inc."

Due authorship credit must be given on all programs, printing and advertising for the play.

PRINTED IN U. S. A.

THE WALTZ OF THE TOREADORS
STORY OF THE PLAY

This outstanding success from the pen of Jean Anouilh —considered by many to be the greatest of European playwrights—is high comedy, exciting, funny, ironic, and cruel. It concerns General St. Pé, quite a soldier and lover in his day; his wife, who spends all her time in bed abusing him roundly; two very plain daughters who bore him to tears; his secretary, a priggish young man who wakes up to the pleasures of love; Mlle. de St.-Euverte, who has guarded her virtue for years following a waltz with the General and who returns to claim him; Dr. Bonfant, the General's great friend and enemy; a flirtatious dressmaker; and others. The General, who can bring himself to do all things except injure his wife, evades the issue of Mlle. de St.-Euverte, who in despair turns to the young secretary. The long consultations between Dr. Bonfant and the General's wife prove to be not entirely medical in scope—and so it goes.

NOTE

The music referred to in this play is copyrighted and may not be used unless permission is granted by, and music rental payments made in advance to Samuel French, Inc. This music is available in recorded form and may be rented from Samuel French, Inc., on a rental fee of $10.00 per performance. A deposit of $30.00 is required on the 5 record set before shipping. We require that these records be sent by express collect and covered by at least $50.00 insurance. The express charges are to be paid both ways by the producing group. If this music is used only in part, or in any other live or recorded form the rental fee is not refundable.

THE WALTZ OF THE TOREADORS

Comedy in three acts by Jean Anouilh, adapted by Lucienne Hill; staged by Harold Clurman; designed by Ben Edwards; presented by the Producers' Theatre at the Coronet Theatre, New York, January 17, 1957, with the following cast:

MME. ST. PÉ	*Mildred Natwick*
GENERAL ST. PÉ	*Ralph Richardson*
GASTON, THE SECRETARY	*John Stewart*
SIDONIA	*Mary Grace Canfield*
ESTELLE	*Sudie Bond*
DR. BONFANT	*John Abbott*
FIRST MAID	*Frieda Altman*
MLLE. DE STE-EUVERTE	*Meriel Forbes*
MME. DUPONT-FREDAINE	*Louise Kirtland*
FATHER AMBROSE	*William Hansen*
NEW MAID	*Helen Seamon*

SCENES

The action of the play takes place in the study of General St. Pé, and in his wife's adjoining bedroom (one unit set).

ACT ONE
SCENE 1: *The Study; a spring afternoon.*
SCENE 2: *The Study; a few minutes later.*

ACT TWO
SCENE 1: *The Study; a few minutes later.*
SCENE 2: *The Bedroom; immediately following.*

ACT THREE
The Study; evening.

The Waltz of the Toreadors

ACT ONE

Scene 1

The GENERAL's room adjoining his wife's bedroom. Two platforms and two sets of double doors Up Center. The inner set is screen doors, leading on the Left to staircase down to the garden. The outer set of wooden double doors leads to dining room and other rooms of the house. A door Up Left Center leads to the bedroom, the front wall of which is a scrim piece, and the Left side wall removable when a scene is to be played in bedroom. Windows in Right wall. A door Down Left to morning room. Exotic trophies, weapons, hangings. The communicating door to the bedroom is open. The GENERAL is at his desk, Left Center, writing and sipping coffee. A shrill VOICE issues from next door.

GENERAL'S WIFE. (*Off*) Leon!
GENERAL. Yes!
VOICE. What are you doing?
GENERAL. Working.
    VOICE. (*Through transparency—from bedroom*). Liar. You are thinking. I can hear you. What are you thinking about?
GENERAL. You.
    VOICE. Liar. You are thinking about women being beautiful and warm, and good to touch, and not feeling all alone in the world for a while, you told me so once.
    GENERAL. I haven't the faintest recollection of it. Go to sleep, my love. You will be tired later.

VOICE. I am only tired, only ill, because of you! Ill with thinking, always thinking of all the things I know you are doing.

GENERAL. Come now, my love, you exaggerate, as usual. (*Stops writing and considers.*) The whole time you have been ill—and that makes years now, I haven't left this room, sitting here glued to this chair dictating my memoirs, or pacing about like a bear in a cage, and well you know it. (*Writes.*)

VOICE. I fell ill with thinking of all the things you are busy doing in your head while you pretend to comfort me. Admit it, hypocrite! Where were you just now in your head? With what woman? In which kitchen, tumbling Heaven knows what drab that scrubs away there on all fours? And you creep up on her like a great tomcat. Leon, you make me sick!

GENERAL. By Hades, Madam, you are dreaming! I am sitting at my desk, writing to the Minister of Foreign Affairs, M. Poincarè.

VOICE. He's a good excuse, Poincarè. You are holding your pen, oh, yes, but in your head your hands are still mauling that girl. Stop it, Leon, if you don't want my death on your conscience. Have you no shame, man, no refinement?

GENERAL. (*Stops writing.*) Will you let me finish my letter in peace?

VOICE. But inside! Inside your head! Why won't you let me inside your head, just once—just for a minute?

GENERAL. (*Puts pen down.*) Confound it, Madam, my head is out of bounds! It's the one spot where I can have a bit of peace, I want it to myself.

VOICE. I shall get into it one day. I shall come upon you there when you least expect it and I shall kill you!

GENERAL. All right. In the meantime—you have brought it on yourself—I shall take Dr. Bonfant's advice and shut the door. (*Rises and crosses Up Center to bedroom door.*)

VOICE. Leon, I forbid you! Leon, I shall have an attack!

ACT I　　WALTZ OF THE TOREADORS　　7

(*In spite of her shrieks the* GENERAL *closes the door. The* SECRETARY *enters through double doors in the course of this punitive expedition, with pad and pencil, and stands Up Center.*)

GENERAL. (*At bedroom door.*) Implacable! I have shut her door! My word, she needn't think I'm going to put up with her whims forever. Good morning, my boy.

SECRETARY. Good morning, sir! (*Crosses to Right desk chair—sits, puts book on desk.*)

GENERAL. (*Crosses Left above desk.*) Haven't you a wife, young man? A little girl friend—it's the old, old story—(*Sits desk chair.*)—you meet her by chance, you take her under the appletrees, and ten minutes later you are married and living with her poor old mother.

SECRETARY. I am too young. (*Rises—opens desk drawer—*GENERAL *hands him manuscript, closes drawer.*)

GENERAL. Yes, and in a flash you'll be too old. You'll be sitting at your desk dictating your memoirs. And between the two, pouff—a game of dice. You must feel the urge sometimes though, I hope? (GENERAL *folds letter—puts it in envelope.*)

SECRETARY. No sir. I have not long left the seminary. I am still chaste.

GENERAL. Good. Sad though. Life without women, my boy, what hell! There's another problem M. Poincarè will never solve. (*Seals letter—puts by* SECRETARY.) Now then, to work. Where were we?

SECRETARY. We have finished Chapter 30. Do you wish me to read it back to you, sir?

GENERAL. Not now. I'm feeling in form. (*Rises—strolls Right.*) I managed to slip out for ten minutes earlier for a turn around the garden. The air was heavy with the scent of rhododendrons—I wandered down a path, it was cool, my joints were as sprightly as a two year old's—nobody called me—it was extraordinary. I fancied I was a widower. Chapter 31. My African Campaigns. Paragraph One. (*Crosses Left Center—Upstage.*) Morocco. Until 1898, the policy of the French Government in

Morocco was a policy of presence. (*Crosses Down Left to globe.*) Since the ill-starred treaty of Frankfurt, however, another factor was coming to have a dangerous bearing on Moroccan policy; the creation of the German Empire whose intrigues and promises were to induce the Sultan to stiffen his attitude towards ourselves. (*Crosses Up to desk.*) An incident, (*Sits desk.*) to all appearances insignificant, was to set a light to the powder.

(*Enter* ESTELLE *and* SIDONIA, *Up Center doors. Lanky wenches of rising 20, still childish, ringletted, kiss-curled and wearing ridiculous little-girl dresses.*)

SIDONIA. (*Left of* ESTELLE.) Papa! (*Crosses to Right Center.*)

GENERAL. Yes.

SIDONIA. What are we going to do about Corpus Christi?

GENERAL. Nothing! We'll say we forgot.

ESTELLE. (*Steps Left to* SIDONIA. *Demanding.*) But Papa, Father Ambrose wants Sidonia and me in white, he said so again yesterday. And we've nothing to wear.

GENERAL. Then wear nothing. It will be fifty times more jolly. Now then, my boy, where were we?

SECRETARY. (*As the* GIRLS *look at each other.*) Relations between the Sultan and the government.

ESTELLE. (*Crosses Down Left of* SIDONIA, *who clears Up Right of* SECRETARY.) Papa! We are carrying the first banner in the procession directly behind the altarboys. We are your daughters and if we don't look as nice as all the other girls, people will talk.

GENERAL. People will talk anyway. Wear your last year's dresses!

SIDONIA. They are too short. We've grown.

GENERAL. Again? Hells bells and little fishes, when are you going to stop? Look at me— (*Rises.*) Have I grown?

ESTELLE. People go on growing until the age of 25.

GENERAL. (*Crosses to them—shoos them Up Center.*) They do in theory. But if they have a scrap of tact they

ACT I WALTZ OF THE TOREADORS 9

leave off sooner. Go and put on your last year's dresses and come and show them to me.

GIRLS. Yes, Papa. (*They go.* SIDONIA *first—Up Center doors.*)

GENERAL. (*Looking at them. Turns front—at screen doors.*) My God, aren't they ugly? (*Crossing Left.*) To think that I, with such a soft spot for a pretty face, could have brought those into the world.

SECRETARY. The misses Saint-Pé are full of all sorts of moral qualities.

GENERAL. (*At desk—sits.*) All sorts, but not the right sort. Heigh-ho—where were we?

SECRETARY. Relations between the Sultan and the Government.

GENERAL. Well now, they weren't going so well either. One fine day the black bastard makes off with a couple of our missionaries. He has a bit of fun with them first and then sends them back, dead as pork, trussed up like sausages minus one or two spare parts. I won't dwell on the ironic element. It was an insult to the flag. The Dubreuil expedition is decided on. Ah, my boy, what a campaign! We got our money's worth for our two priests! By jingo, we ran through some Arabs! With good clean steel too and no nonsense. And then, my boy, the little girls of twelve, the way they grow 'em in those parts—wonderful! There she is, terror stricken, crouching naked in a corner, a little creature that knows it will be forced, and that desires it almost. Two young breasts, tender as fawns, and cruppers, me lad!—And eyes! And you the soldier, the conqueror, the master. Your sword still steaming in your hand—you have killed—you are all-powerful—she knows it and you know it too—it is hot and dark inside the tent, and there you stand, face to face, in silence—

SECRETARY. (*Flushed and panting. Leans forward.*) And then, sir?

GENERAL. (*Simply.*) Well, dammit all, at that age! We're not savages. We turned them over to the Sisters of Mercy at Rabat. (*Enter* DOCTOR BONFANT *with bag, up staircase—through screen doors. Crosses Down Right Center above sofa.*) Ah, here's Dr. Bonfant come to see his patient. Leave us for a while, my boy. I shall ring for you. Good morning, Doctor.

SECRETARY. Good morning.

DOCTOR. Good morning. (*The* SECRETARY *picks up his papers and with pad, pencil and letter, exits Up Center doors. The* GENERAL *watches him go.*) Good day to you, General. (*Crosses Left to Center.*)

GENERAL. Fine-looking young chap, isn't he? Would have cut quite a dash as a dragoon but for his vocation as a virgin. (*Shakes hands.*) Superb handwriting though, and no fool. (*Shows manuscript, and puts in drawer.*) The Curé found him for me. He's a parish child one of his colleagues brought up.

DOCTOR. And how is our invalid this morning?

GENERAL. The same as yesterday, the same as tomorrow, no doubt. And how is medical science progressing?

DOCTOR. (*Crosses Right—to Right desk chair.*) No further. We have found other terms far less vague than the old ones to designate the same complaints. (*Sits Right chair.*) It's a great advance linguistically. No scenes today? (*Puts bag down on floor.*)

GENERAL. A small one on the usual theme. However, I took your advice and shut the door.

DOCTOR. Excellent. And did that silence her?

GENERAL. She must have gone on on the other side but at least I couldn't hear her.

DOCTOR. As I say, this paralysis of the lower limbs is of a purely nervous origin, like all the rest. The mental process is quite simple—we won't walk any more so as to arouse his pity and make it impossible for him to leave us. You must have led her a dance to have brought her to that, General.

GENERAL. Not to that extent, Doctor, not to that extent. I loved my wife very much at first. Yes, it seems as odd to me now as my craze over a stamp collection at fifteen. But it's a fact, we had a few happy years—well, when I say happy. . . . Before lapsing into bigotry and fruitbottling, Emily had quite an amorous disposition. My wife was an opera singer, you know. She bellowed her way through Wagner as a Walkyrie. I married her and made her give up the theatre, to my eternal cost. She was to go on acting for myself alone. A performance at his own expense, lasting for more than twenty years, tends to wear out your spectator. So I set about finding my fun elsewhere, naturally. Chambermaids, waitresses—(*Takes cigar box.*) whatever hole-and-corner capers a man dares to indulge in, who is very closely watched. And I grew old, little by little. First a shade too much stomach, then the paunch advancing as the hair recedes, and the sleeve wound round with more and more gold string. (*Offers cigar to* DOCTOR *who refuses.*) And beneath this fancy dress the heart of an aged youngster still waiting for a chance to give his all. But who's to recognize me underneath the mask?

DOCTOR. What would you say if I told you more or less the same tale, General?

GENERAL. (*Lights cigar.*) It wouldn't be the slightest consolation. At least your wife didn't decide at the eleventh hour to fall madly in love with you and die of unrequited passion.

DOCTOR. She makes up for it in other ways. (*Rising, takes bag.*) Well now, I shall go and take her blood pressure. That won't do her any harm. It is always normal anyway. (*Crosses Up Left to bedroom.*) Does she eat at all?

GENERAL. (*Crosses Right below screen door.*) Like you or me. I shall make the most of your visit and take a little turn around the garden, like any carefree bachelor. Don't tell her, she would accuse me of deceiving her with a geranium. (DOCTOR *enters bedroom,* GENERAL *goes out Up Center doors.*)

(*The stage is empty for a moment. The* SECRETARY *is heard outside singing an Italian love song. The* MAID *shows in a* VISITOR *from stairs, a woman decked out in furs and feathers, and swathed in travelling veils.*)

MAID. (*Leading her to Center.*) It's very early, Madam. I think the master is taking his morning stroll around the garden.

GHISLAINE. Is that he singing? It sounds like his voice. (*Crosses Right to window.*)

MAID. Oh no, Madam. That's the Secretary. I'll go and ask the master if he will receive you, Madam.

GHISLAINE. (*Turns.*) Mademoiselle.

MAID. I beg your pardon, Mademoiselle. What name shall I say?

GHISLAINE. Mademoiselle de Ste-Euverte.

MAID. Very good, Mademoiselle. (*The MAID goes out—Up Center doors.*)

GHISLAINE. (*Makes a tour of the room, touching things with her sunshade. Crosses Left Center to desk—turns.*) Nothing has changed in this house. (*She runs her finger along the desk top.*) Still as much dust as ever. The poor darling needs someone badly. (*Crosses Right to Center—above chair. She listens to the song and murmurs.*) Strange—it sounds so like his voice. (*The song stops.*)

GENERAL. (*Runs upstairs, appears in the doorway, and stops, dumbfounded.*) Ghislaine!

GHISLAINE. (*Near bedroom door.*) Leon!

GENERAL. You here?

GHISLAINE. Yes. And with head held high.

GENERAL. There'll be the devil of a row.

GHISLAINE. I came so that it might take place.

GENERAL. (*Right of her. Terrified.*) Careful. She's in that room.

GHISLAINE. Alone?

GENERAL. (*Takes her Down Center.*) Doctor Bonfant is with her.

GHISLAINE. I thought as much. (*He looks at her questioningly.*) I'll explain in a minute. First let me look at you. (*He stands Up Right of her below sofa, she opens veil.*) Leon!

GENERAL. Ghislaine! You!

GHISLAINE. Myself.

ACT I WALTZ OF THE TOREADORS 13

GENERAL. As intrepid as an Amazon!

GHISLAINE. (*Crosses Right a step.*) I took the night express. I found myself alone in the compartment with a fellow of sinister aspect who was pretending to read a newspaper.

GENERAL. (*A step Left and anxiously.*) Ghislaine—

GHISLAINE. At one point he asked me the time.

GENERAL. (*Backs a step.*) The swine!

GHISLAINE. But I gave him such a look that he took the hint immediately. He even said thank you as if I really had told him the time. He folded his newspaper and fell asleep. Or perhaps he was only pretending. But I was perfectly calm—I was armed. See, this little revolver with the mother-of-pearl handle which you may remember, Leon. (*Takes it from her reticule—looks at it and caresses it.*)

GENERAL. Ghislaine, you have it still?

GHISLAINE. Had he made one false move, had he so much as touched the hem of my dress I would have slain him first and myself afterwards—I had to get to you intact. (*Returns gun to bag.*)

GENERAL. (*Sits Right end sofa pulling her down Left of him.*) Thank you, Ghislaine. But you know it's impossible, Ghislaine.

GHISLAINE. Everything is possible now. I have the proof of it here in my reticule. Our long years of waiting will not have been in vain, Leon.

GENERAL. Seventeen years . . .

GHISLAINE. Seventeen years since the Garrison Ball at Saumur.

GENERAL. The Chinese lanterns, Ghislaine, the gypsy orchestra— The Colonel thought it too daring but I stood my ground. They had been sent for all the way from Paris.

GHISLAINE. Oh the strange enchantment of that first waltz, Leon!

GENERAL. (*Rises, crosses Left of her—turns.*) **The Waltz of the Toreadors.**

GHISLAINE. Tra la la, la la la.

GENERAL. (*Hand out.*) Mademoiselle, may I have the pleasure?

GHISLAINE. (*Looks at imaginary card.*) But, sir, you are not on my card.

GENERAL. (*Simulates writing.*) I will inscribe myself on it officially. Major St. Pé. We have not been introduced but I feel that I have known you all my life.

GHISLAINE. (*Rises—turns to him. Coyly.*) Why Major, how bold you are! Then you took me by the waist and all at once your hand burned me right through your gloves and my dress. From the moment your hand touched my back I no longer heard the music. Everything whirled . . . (*She twirls Left to desk.*)

GENERAL. The waltz! Tra la la la—Tra la la— (*He takes her in his arms and begins to waltz with her.*)

GHISLAINE. (*Swooning.*) It was love! Tra la la la—

(ESTELLE *and* SIDONIA *appear in Up Center doorway,* SIDONIA *at Right, in their overshort white dresses.*)

SIDONIA. (*Crosses to Right Center.*) Papa, we've come about the dresses.

GENERAL. (*Hastily releases his partner and steps Up Left above desk.*) Ten thousand demons, can't you see I'm busy? This lady is my teacher. I am having a dancing lesson. (GHISLAINE *turns away below desk.*)

ESTELLE. Is there to be a ball then, Papa?

GENERAL. (*Improvising wildly.*) Yes! I'm arranging one. For Corpus Christi, funnily enough. (*Introducing them.*) My daughters. (*They curtsy.*)

GHISLAINE. Is it possible? Those darling little babies!

GENERAL. (*Strugging.*) There we are.

GHISLAINE. But it was only yesterday?

GENERAL. They shot up very fast. You see, (*Touches* ESTELLE'S *dress.*) they've already grown out of their new dresses. This lady is an old friend who saw you when you were tiny. As for the dresses, it's clear you both want new ones. Granted. Run along to Mme. Dupont-Fredaine, choose the stuff—

ACT I   WALTZ OF THE TOREADORS   15

THE GIRLS. (*Clapping their hands.*) Oh thank you, Papa, darling Papa!

GENERAL. —and tell her to come and see me about terms no later than this afternoon. (*Shooing them Up Center.*)

ESTELLE. (*They step up—turn to him.*) Thank you, papa.

SIDONIA. We'll look lovely after all, Papa.

GENERAL. Well, we'll have a shot at it anyhow. (*The* GIRLS *skip out hand in hand at Up Center doors.*) What a pair of silly geese! Heaven knows what tales they're going to spread. (*At bedroom door.*)

GHISLAINE. (*Right below sofa. In a strangely altered voice.*) But why are they so big? Leon, can I have aged as well?

GENERAL. (*Crosses Down Right Center.*) You are still the same Ghislaine, the same beautiful tuber rose wafting her night-time fragrance over the gardens of Saumur!

GHISLAINE. (*Sits sofa.*) But I was eighteen years old at that ball!

GENERAL. It never does to start adding up. (*Taking her hand.*) Your hand! (*Sits Left of her.*) Your little hand imprisoned in its glove. Do you remember that meringue at Rumpelmeyers seven years ago?

GHISLAINE. No. You're wrong. The whole of 1904 we couldn't meet at all. It was the beginning of her attacks. The meringue was 1903.

GENERAL. I ate the little bits from off your fingers.

GHISLAINE. You were as bold as brass even then. Yet we had only known each other a few years.

GENERAL. Why count the years? It was a week ago. Your fingers still smell of meringue.

MAID. (*Enters up the stairs.*) Excuse me, sir.

GENERAL. (*Starting.*) Yes—what?

MAID. (*Crossing Down Center—Left of him.*) The new one's come, sir.

GENERAL. The new what?

MAID. The new girl to replace Justine.

GENERAL. Suffering catfish! Can't you see I'm busy?

I haven't time to go on choosing chambermaids. Engage her— (*She starts Up Center—he stops her.*) What does she look like? (*Crosses Up Center to Right of her.*)

MAID. A fine looking girl, sir, dark and a little on the plump side.

GENERAL. (*Dreamily.*) A little on the plump side. . . . Engage her.

(*The* MAID *goes out Up Center.*)

GHISLAINE. Leon, I wish you would let me help you. (*He turns to her.*) You don't know what you may be getting.

GENERAL. Thank you, Ghislaine, but there's no need. (*Sits Left of her.*) From what I hear she's sure to be very nice. Besides, we have decisions to make. Your presence here is unthinkable, my love, you know that.

GHISLAINE. This time, though, I am quite determined to stay.

GENERAL. What did you say?

GHISLAINE. (*Solemnly. Rises—a step Right.*) Leon, I have waited for so long in silence, keeping myself for you. If I were to bring you positive proof of the unworthiness of her for whom we sacrificed ourselves, what would you do? (*Turns to him.*)

GENERAL. Unworthiness? Emily unworthy? Alas, Ghislaine, you must be dreaming.

GHISLAINE. (*Facing front.*) Yes, Leon, I am dreaming, dreaming that I am about to live at last! (*Turning to him—putting reticule to her bosom.*) In this reticule I hold clasped to my heart I have two letters. Two letters signed by her hand. Two love letters to a man.

GENERAL. (*Rises.*) Thundering canonballs, it can't be true!

GHISLAINE. (*Crosses Left to him. On his bosom.*) We are free, Leon!

GENERAL. (*Pushes her Right.*) Who is it? I demand to know his name!

GHISLAINE. It's Doctor Bonfant. (*Points to bedroom.*)

GENERAL. Dr. Bonfant!

DOCTOR. (*Enters, beaming. Crosses Down Center with bag.*) Ah, General! I am happy to be able to tell you that she is much better today. (GENERAL *glares.*) We chatted for a while and that appeared to soothe her. You see how wrong you are to poke fun at doctoring. (GENERAL *advances to him.*) It all depends on the doctor, and the way one goes about it. (*Pokes him in stomach.*)

GENERAL. (*Icily.*) No need to labor the point, Doctor. There is a young lady present. (*The* DOCTOR *turns to* GHISLAINE *in mild surprise.*)

DOCTOR. I do beg your pardon. (*Bowing.*) Madame.

GHISLAINE. (*With infinite nobility.*) Mademoiselle. But not for very long now!

(*The* DOCTOR *straightens, astonished.*)

CURTAIN

ACT ONE

SCENE 2

The same. The GENERAL *and* DOCTOR *are alone. The latter seated, the* GENERAL *pacing feverishly about the room.*

GENERAL. (*Down Right.*) Swords—Sir— What do you say to swords? (*Crosses Left to Center.*)

DOCTOR. (*Seated Right desk chair.*) General, I say you are quite wrong.

GENERAL. (*Paces Center.*) Blood must be shed, sir! I shall listen to your explanations afterwards.

DOCTOR. It may be a trifle late by then.

GENERAL. (*Crosses Down Right Center.*) I can't help that. Blood to begin with, sir!

DOCTOR. You're quite right. With the present state of

your arteries. . . . How about a little cut with the lancet first? I have my bag here.

GENERAL. Your sawbones humour is uncalled for, sir.

DOCTOR. I am quite serious. Blood pressure is our triumph. It is one of the few chances we have of being accurate, thanks to our little gadget here. That is why we take it on every conceivable occasion. The last time you were up to 250. That's very high, you know.

GENERAL. (*Crosses Down Right.*) I don't care, sir. I shall consult one of your colleagues. It is a question of honor at the moment. (*After a pause turns Center.*) 250, is that high?

DOCTOR. Very.

GENERAL. (*After another slight pause, crosses Left a step.*) Did you or did you not receive those letters?

DOCTOR. I tell you I never did. If I had, how could they come to be in your possession?

GENERAL. True enough. . . . You've seen them though. They aren't forgeries.

DOCTOR. (*Puzzled.*) Apparently not.

GENERAL. Therefore, sir, the fact is this: my wife is in love with you.

DOCTOR. (*Puts bag down.*) So she writes.

GENERAL. And you consider that perfectly normal, do you?

DOCTOR. (*Almost laughs.*) What can I do about it?

GENERAL. (*Paces Up Center.*) By jove, sir, has the Medical Corps no honor! Any cadet—what am I saying?—any regular NCO would already have replied: At your service! (*Crosses Down Center and Right.*) Explanations would have followed later. How would you like it if I slapped your face? (*Turns to him.*)

DOCTOR. I should promptly slap you back, sir. And there I should have the advantage of you. I am Acting President of the Sports Club of which you are merely the Honorary Secretary. (*Rises.*) I do an hour's exercise every morning. You spoke about your paunch just now. We are the same age. Just look at mine. (*Crosses **Right Center** to him. He lets his trousers down.*)

GENERAL. (*Grudgingly.*) You're pulling it in.

DOCTOR. No. Feel it. It's quite natural. (*Crosses Right a step.*) Now look at yours.

GENERAL. (*Undoes his own trousers and examines his figure.*) Holy Moses!

DOCTOR. Go on, feel. Feel mine. Now feel yours.

GHISLAINE. (*Appears Down Left in the doorway of the morning room.*) You're wounded! (*Crosses to Right end of desk.*)

(*The DOCTOR and the GENERAL hastily pull up trousers.*)

GENERAL. (*Crosses Down Left to her.*) No, no of course not. Go back into the morning room, and don't come out whatever you do. We will call you when it's all over. (*He propels her into the morning room, and completes the adjustments to his dress.*) What a business! (*Steps below Left chair.*)

DOCTOR. (*Crossing Left Center buttoning trousers.*) I am all at sea, I must confess. Who is this young woman?

GENERAL. (*Buttoning.*) Young girl, sir, a friend of mine. I forbid you to jump to any conclusions.

DOCTOR. If I cannot even form a supposition I shall be more at sea than ever. Who is she? (*Both sit. GENeral Left of desk, DOCTOR Right.*)

GENERAL. (*Both finish buttoning.*) Mlle. de Ste-Euverte—a lady descended from one of the noblest houses of Lorraine—is the love of my life, Doctor, and I am hers. I met her at the annual Ball of the Eighth Dragoons at Saumur in 1893, seventeen years ago. She was a girl of the best society, I was a married man. Anything between us was quite out of the question. At the time, owing to my career and the children, I dared not contemplate divorce. And yet we could not give up our love.

DOCTOR. So she became your mistress!

GENERAL. No, sir! I respected her maidenhood. Seventeen years that's been going on! Mlle. de Ste-Euverte is still a maiden and I am still a prisoner.

DOCTOR. But dammit, General, your career is established, your daughters are grown up, what in Heaven are you waiting for?

GENERAL. I'll tell you a secret, Doctor, a miserable secret. I am a coward.

DOCTOR. Stuff and nonsense, General! You wanted to run me through a minute ago. And what about your oakleaves and your eighteen wounds?

GENERAL. (*Simply.*) Those were done to me. It's not the same. Besides, in battle it's comparatively simple. Life is a different thing. (*A pause. He says dully.*) I can't make people suffer. (*Rises, crosses Down Right.*)

DOCTOR. (*Gently.*) Then you will make them suffer a great deal, my friend, and you will suffer a great deal yourself.

GENERAL. (*Right of* DOCTOR.) I fear so.

DOCTOR. Let us sum up the situation, shall we? I want to help you out of this dilemma. You are in love with this young woman.

GENERAL. (*Center—turns to* DOCTOR.) Young girl, sir.

DOCTOR. Young girl, if you prefer it. She loves you. She has spent years waiting for you. She sacrificed her youth in vain anticipation of a happiness which you once promised her. You owe her that happiness now.

GENERAL. (*Crosses Right to sofa.*) I know. Not a minute has gone by during those seventeen years that has not been poisoned by the thought of it. (*Sits.*) What is she doing? She is alone, playing the piano in the deserted drawing room of her big house, doing her embroidery, eating alone at her vast table in the chilly dining room where my place is always laid and always vacant. I know it, sir, I know it all. (*Crosses Up Left Center to gun on wall.*) Time and again I have seized my service revolver —I'm not afraid of death—he's an old comrade—bang-bang, all over. For me, not for her. I had no right to do it. (*Crosses Down Right—Sits Left end sofa.*)

DOCTOR. (*Rises, crosses Right to* GENERAL.) Leave your revolver, like your sword, up on the wall, General.

Among all your military equipment did you never think of your kitbag?

GENERAL. My kitbag?

DOCTOR. Two shirts, three pairs of pants, six handkerchiefs, hey presto, and Mademoiselle de Ste-Euverte is no longer—a mademoiselle!

GENERAL. And my wife, sir?

DOCTOR. Do you love her?

GENERAL. Lord, no! But she loves me. She'll die of it.

DOCTOR. (*Crosses Up to Left of desk.*) Hum, I wonder. Women have unexpected reserves. I understand she wrote to say she was in love with me. (*Leans on Right desk chair.*)

GENERAL. (*Leaping up, crosses Left to* DOCTOR.) Upon my soul, sir, how dare you! You have offended me. To the sword, sir! To the sword!

DOCTOR. (*Crosses to him.*) Now General, we must try to understand each other. If you kill a man for her sake, I can't see you anywhere near to leaving her. You must be logical, General.

GENERAL. (*Looks in his eyes.*) Can you swear that you are not her lover?

DOCTOR. On the head of my wife.

GENERAL. (*Crosses Down Right—sits sofa.*) Anyway she's ugly—nothing but a bag of bones.

DOCTOR. Oh no, General, your wife was never what one would call a beauty, but when you came to live here fifteen years ago, I don't mind telling you, my dear fellow, that she created quite a stir. (GENERAL *starts.*) Not in me, sir, not in me—particularly! But her personality, her clothes, her talent. . . . Very attractive woman, sir, was your wife—and then, coming from Paris as she did . . . (*Leans Down Right corner of desk.*)

GENERAL. She comes from Carpentras.

DOCTOR. She had just come from Paris (*Crosses to Right Center.*) nonetheless, and from the opera. You know what they are in the provinces. I am personally acquainted with two who at all events cherished secret hopes.

GENERAL. (*Awful in his anger.*) Their names!

DOCTOR. (*Up Left of* GENERAL.) What is the use General, now? One of them is in a wheel chair through sacrificing overmuch to Venus. The other is dead.

GENERAL. Always too late.

DOCTOR. Exactly. The more I think of it, General, the more I am disturbed by your case. This constant living in the past—

GENERAL. I know. I forget my paunch and the gold strings on my sleeve. I am old.

DOCTOR. (*Left of* GENERAL.) Your jealousy of Madam St. Pé was fine in the old tooth-and-nail days. What can it possibly matter to you now? Your love for Mademoiselle de Ste-Euverte was for Mademoiselle de Ste-Euverte as a young girl, the night of the garrison ball. That one has been dead these many years. Neither you nor she herself can so much as recall what she once was.

GENERAL. (*With a disarming smile.*) Oh yes, Doctor, dear me yes!

DOCTOR. A tender memory. The memory of a dead girl. And Major St. Pé is dead too. Turn your attention to your rose trees. (*Pointing toward window Down Right.*) You haven't so much longer, you know. Why not forget him?

GENERAL. (*Rises, crosses Down Right to window, turns Left.*) Never! The heart has stayed the same, sir, under the ironmongery. (*Springing to attention.*) Lieutenant St. Pé! Graduated second from Saumur! No money, but plenty of courage and well thought of! Ready to give his all for France, for honour, for a woman! A real woman, sweet and loving, faithful and pure; not that third-rate prima donna. I am thirty years old. I swear I am. And I did find that woman. I found her last night, at the Annual Ball at Saumur. I am ready.

DOCTOR. (*Crosses Right toward him above sofa.*) Then you must make haste, General. One good honest explanation. Cut to the quick before gangrene sets in. Hurt if you must but do it without flinching. And then start again afresh. Crossing the threshold of that door seems like flying to the moon, but in fact all it requires is this one step. (*Stands above sofa.*)

GHISLAINE. (*Appears at the door Down Left. Crosses to Center.*) I can't stand it! I must know!

GENERAL. (*Slightly on edge. Crosses Left to her.*) Dammit all, Ghislaine, you've waited seventeen years, surely you can contain yourself for an extra ten minutes!

GHISLAINE. No I can't, not even for ten minutes.

GENERAL. I must have time enough to make her confess, and inform her of my irrevocable decision. She is an invalid, dammit. I owe her some consideration. Don't you be cruel, too.

GHISLAINE. I bore her cruelty and respected her love so long as I believed her faithful to you. Now I know that she dared to betray you I shall know no pity, Leon, and no patience. Either way, should you be capable of hesitating still, I have a little revolver with a mother of pearl handle which you may remember, here in my reticule. I shall end this life within the hour, without ever having known more of love than your vain promises, Leon.

GENERAL. (*Sags.*) Give me strength! All I ask is a moment to set my life in order. (*Propels her Left.*) Go back into the morning room and be patient. There are some magazines on the table.

GHISLAINE. (*Stops at door—turns Right.*) Magazines! Like at the dentist's! You have wounded me for the first time, my dear.

GENERAL. (*Crosses Right to her.*) My beloved! Who said anything about a dentist? Anyhow you aren't the one who is going to have the tooth out. Just one moment. I adore you! (*He pushes her gently but firmly back into the morning room.*)

DOCTOR. General! (*Points to bedroom.*)

GENERAL. Yes! Time is getting on. Suppose you spoke to her first, Doctor? (*Crosses to bedroom door—stops—turns to DOCTOR.*)

DOCTOR. (*Crosses Left to him.*) That might prove a little awkward considering those letters. Suppose she falls into my arms? There'll be no end of explaining to do then.

GENERAL. That's true. Stay here though, will you, and if I cry out "Help" come in. (*Knocks on door, then he goes into his wife's room, and rushes out again almost at once, distractedly waving a letter. Crosses Down Center.*) Doctor, she's not in her room!

DOCTOR. (*Starts and crosses Up Center to him.*) Good heavens! Is there another way out?

GENERAL. Through the window, by hanging on to the wistaria.

DOCTOR. In her condition—

GENERAL. (*Both cross Down Center.* DOCTOR *Right.*) She left this letter on the table.—"I heard everything. Men are all cowards. Whatever they may have said to you, Leon, I have never loved anyone but you. I can walk when I want to. I am going. You will never hear of me again." Good God! Does she mean she wants to kill herself?

DOCTOR. (*Looking at his watch.*) The railroad crossing! She spoke of it! The train goes through at five past! It's two minutes to.

GENERAL. The pond! You go one way—I'll go the other! (*They both rush out.* GENERAL *downstairs—*DOCTOR *Up Center doors.* GHISLAINE *comes in almost at once Down Left.*)

GHISLAINE. (*Crosses to Right above desk.*) I too heard everything. You love her still, Leon! (*With determination.*) Only one way out. (*She sits at the desk and begins to write rapidly, calm but dabbing away a tear through her veil. Murmuring.*) Leon, here is my last letter to you— (*Her voice trails away, she continues to write.* GASTON, *the secretary, is heard outside the window, singing his Italian love song. The ditty continues throughout the writing of the letter. When she has finished,* GHISLAINE *leaves it on the* GENERAL'S *desk in a prominent position.*) There. On his books. That's all. It's the simplest thing in the world. (*She rises unhurriedly, picks up her reticule, draws out the revolver with the mother*

ACT I   **WALTZ OF THE TOREADORS**   25

of pearl handle, presses it to her heart, and pulls the trigger. Nothing happens. She looks at the gun in surprise, pulls out a catch, pushes another, blows into the barrel, puts to her head. Left finger in ear, and fires again. Still nothing. Sighing. Looks at it—clicks it—then.) You too have been waiting seventeen years. (*She throws the gun into waste basket, looks at her fob-watch and mutters.*) Too late for the train. The pond! (*Crosses Down Center but changes her mind.*) No. Not in the same place as her, for Heaven's sake! (*She darts a quick look round the room.*) The window! With a little luck . . . (*Crosses Up Right. She takes a run at it, steps up on edge and drops. The singing ends abruptly in a loud hiccup.*)

MAID. (*Ad-libs off stage.*) For Goodness sakes—what was that? Who screamed that way? What's the matter—what happened? Someone go fetch the master quickly—oh! (*The stage is empty for a moment, then* SECRETARY *enters up the stairs carrying a senseless* GHISLAINE, *closely followed by the* MAID.) Goodness gracious sir, whatever's the matter? You yelled fit to raise the dead!

SECRETARY. (*Crosses Down Right Center. Puts* GHISLAINE *on sofa.*) I was rocking quietly in the hammock when this lady comes tumbling down on my head.

MAID. (*Down Center.*) Well fancy that! Maybe she wanted to kill you?

SECRETARY. (*Turns to her.*) Herself more likely. Besides I don't know her from Adam. She's fainted. (*Turns to* GHISLAINE.)

MAID. And the Doctor just this minute left. The man as good as lives here half the time, and the one day we have a suicide he's out!

SECRETARY. (*Slapping* GHISLAINE'S *face—turns to* MAID.) For God's sake, go and fetch something.

MAID. What?

SECRETARY. Well *I* don't know—ointment, smelling salts—iodine. . . . Anything. (*Turns to* GHISLAINE.)

MAID. I'll make her a good strong cup of coffee. (*She goes downstairs.*)

SECRETARY. No blood, anyway. (*He feels her all over.*) No bones broken, apparently. No bumps. Madame! Madame! (*Kneels—patting her hand.*)

GHISLAINE. (*Weakly.*) Mademoiselle.

SECRETARY. Mademoiselle—I beg your pardon. Are you feeling better?

GHISLAINE. (*Murmuring.*) Leave your hands where they are, Leon.

SECRETARY. (*Removes hand turning away in embarrassment.*) Excuse me, but you are making a mistake.

GHISLAINE. (*Crying out.*) Leave your hands, Leon—caressing me—or I feel I shall swoon again—your hands quickly!—I'm going—

SECRETARY. (*Looking in panic at his hands.*) My hands? Oh dear, I can't very well let her faint away again. Not that it's at all unpleasant, and I am such a lonely young man. Besides I'll mention it when I go to confession. (*Puts hands on her waist.*)

GHISLAINE. Oh, how good it is! You are touching me at last, Leon! You thought me strong—and I was strong—I had to be, but oh, how long they were, all those nights on my own! Before I met you I was alone too, but I never knew it. It was on the morrow of the Summer Ball that my bed suddenly seemed wide—that next night and all the nights for seventeen years. (*Pulls his head down.*) And all the wicked thoughts—you don't know! I shall never tell you. I struggled alone. (*Lets him up.*) No one was to touch me until you finally came. Your arms are strong, and gentle your hands, gentler even than at the Saumur Ball. Kiss me, now that you know I am going to die. What are you waiting for, Leon, my death?

SECRETARY. (*Turns front—wringing hands.*) The lady is obviously making a mistake, but seeing that she may be going to die— (*Rises—bends over and kisses her.*)

GHISLAINE. (*Has the time to sigh.*) At last! (*Pulls him down in sofa, a long kiss.*)

GENERAL. (*Enters carrying his unconscious* WIFE *over his shoulder. He stands rooted to the spot at the sight which confronts him.*) What the hell do you think you're doing?

SECRETARY. (*Jumps up—crosses Down Right and Up Right of sofa in terror.*) But sir, the lady is delirious.

GENERAL. (*Crosses Down Center bawling.*) Fifty thousand devils, I can well believe it! But what about you?

SECRETARY. She fell on top of me, sir, and ordered me to kiss her.

GENERAL. Hells bells, has everyone round here gone mad this morning? (*Still encumbered with his unconscious wife, shouting.*) What's wrong with you? What happened?

SECRETARY. (*Up Right Center.*) She threw herself out of the window, sir. Thank goodness I was underneath in the hammock. She landed right on my head.

GENERAL. (*Turns front.*) Out of the window! Holy Moses, they're insane, the lot of them! My beloved! Here my boy, take my wife, will you? (*He puts his wife into* SECRETARY'S *arms and throws himself down beside* GHISLAINE.) Ghislaine! My dearest! Why did you want to die?

GHISLAINE. (*Coming to.*) Who is that touching me? I do not know those hands.

GENERAL. It's I, Ghislaine, Leon. Your Leon.

GHISLAINE. (*Pushing him away.*) Let me go. You aren't Leon. I don't recognize your hands. (*The* GENERAL *kisses her.*) Nor your mouth. Just now, at long last, Leon kissed me. He is twenty years old. (GENERAL *glares at* SECRETARY, *starts after him, but turns back and puts a hand on* GHISLAINE.) I forbid you to touch me. No one may touch me but him. I am keeping myself.

GENERAL'S WIFE. (*Coming to in the* SECRETARY'S *arms, flapping her arms.*) Leon!

GENERAL. (*Turns.*) That's done it. The other one will come to in a minute. She mustn't see her here. She'd kill herself a second time. (*Picks up* GHISLAINE *and starts to cross Left with her.*)

GENERAL'S WIFE. (*Clinging to the* SECRETARY'S *neck*

and screeching.) Leon, hold me! Kiss me, Leon! You can see I'm dying. Kiss me quickly before I am quite dead!

SECRETARY. (*Yelling in his panic after the* GENERAL *who is carrying* GHISLAINE *away.*) This one wants to be kissed before she dies as well!!! What am I to do?

GENERAL. (*Stops at door Left and turns.*) You must be out of your mind, my boy! Can't you see they're both delirious? Put Madame down in her room. I am taking this young lady in here. (*Kicks door Down Left open with* GHISLAINE'S *feet.* SECRETARY *exits into bedroom with* GENERAL'S WIFE. *The* MAID *comes in with the coffee and stands Center gaping.*)

CURTAIN

ACT TWO

Scene 1

Scene: *The same.*

(*The* General *is alone. He appears to be waiting. The* Doctor *comes out of the morning room.*)

General. (*Seated—sofa Right—with pipe. There are wine bottle and corkscrew on table beside him.*) Well?

Doctor. (*At Down Left door. Crosses up to bed. Puts bag down.*) They are both resting. I gave them a good sedative. The snag is that they will eventually wake up. (*Crosses Down Right Center.*)

General. We are so peaceful as we are! It's most odd, for an hour now there hasn't been a sound. I was even on the point of gathering a few ideas. You know, science ought to find a way of putting women permanently to sleep. We could wake them for a while at night and then they would go back to sleep again.

Doctor. (*Sits Right desk chair.*) But what about the housework? You should see the performance if I have to fry myself an egg! And that's nothing, there's the washing up afterwards.

General. (*Puts corkscrew in wine bottle.*) If the worse came to the worst we wouldn't put the maids to sleep. (Doctor *snaps finger in agreement.*) Have you seen the latest little one? With all these upsets I haven't even had a chance to say hello to her. A bosom, my dear chap! (*Pops cork.*) Dear Lord, how simple it could all be! Why do we complicate life so? (*Pours wine.*)

Doctor. Because we have a soul, General. Take an old freethinker's word for it. It's that which makes life hell for us. (General *hands him a glass of wine.*) The maid's petticoats are pleasant at the time, but afterwards without love, without any real desire—what emptiness.

(*Rises, Crosses Down Right. Sits Down Right chair with wine glass.*) I'll tell you a secret, General. We have all stayed little boys. Only the little girls grow up.

GENERAL. (*Suddenly, points to Left door.*) There is one though, who never hurt me, who never once complained. True, I never lived with her. Oh if you could have seen her at the Saumur Ball! I bet you don't believe that I really love her, having waited all this time?

DOCTOR. My dear man, one must never judge the courage or the love of others. No one can say who loves or is afraid.

GENERAL. (*Rises, crosses to Center with wine.*) There's my life story, Doctor, in a nutshell. The shell is handsome. They have painted the oakleaves onto it, and Lord knows how many decorations. I have a lovely house, splendid whiskers, the easy wenches in these parts refuse me nothing. When I go by on my black mare of a morning, in my corsets, I'll even wager I make the little virgins at the High School that peep behind their curtains dream of me. I utter enormities when the fancy takes me and everyone turns a deaf ear, even the priest, because I have a way with me. Well, my friend, the shell is empty. There's nobody inside. (*Crosses Down Left a step.*) I am alone, and I'm afraid.

DOCTOR. (*Rises.*) Afraid of what? (*Crosses Left to below sofa.*)

GENERAL. (*Sits Right desk chair.*) I dunno. Of my loneliness, I suppose.

DOCTOR. (*With a smile.*) My poor old friend. (*Sits sofa.*)

GENERAL. My bits of fun even, do you think they amuse me? They bore me to death. It is my terror of living which sends me scampering after them. When you see them swinging by with their buttocks and their breasts under their dresses you feel I don't know what wild hope surge up inside you. But once the dress is off and you have to get down to it! The only thing is that with all these philanderings you get to my age realising that you have never in your life made love. It's wrong of

ACT II WALTZ OF THE TOREADORS

me to make fun of my secretary. I am an old virgin, Doctor.

DOCTOR. (*Rises, crosses Left to Right of* GENERAL *with wine.*) No; you have the sickness, General, that's all.

GENERAL. Which one? I've had them all . . .

DOCTOR. Those sicknesses are nothing. (*Crosses Up Left above desk.*) They can be treated. We have a soul, General. I long denied the phenomenon. I was one of the old school; we did not bother with that subject in my day. I wanted to stick to abscesses and cancers. But now I know. It's in the soul the trouble lies, in nine cases out of ten. (*Sits Left desk chair.*)

GENERAL. But dammit all, everybody has a soul! That's no reason for being scared out of one's wits a whole life long. (*Crosses Right—fills wine glass.*)

DOCTOR. It is, General. Souls are rare. And when by ill luck you happen to possess one, if you don't make your peace with it, it's war.

GENERAL. Peace, peace? But what brand of peace does it want, damn its eyes? It surely doesn't expect me to take Holy Orders, does it? (*Puts bottle in bucket Right.*)

DOCTOR. No. If it were as simple as that you would have done it long ago.

GENERAL. (*Crosses Left a step.*) Then what *does* the jade want? The only time I feel slightly at peace is when I look at something beautiful. Dammit, I can't turn myself into a painter or sculptor, can I? What then— (*Crosses to Center.*) scuttling from art gallery to museum like a halfwit, brandishing a Kodak? No, by Heaven! (*Puts wine glass on desk.*) Beauty's a thing one should be able to fashion for oneself.

DOCTOR. What about Mlle. de Ste-Euverte, General?

GENERAL. (*After a pause.*) Well, yes, there it is. You know, it's an extraordinary thing what happened to me at Saumur. There was a girl like any other—the colour of her dress and hair had caught my eye—I introduce myself, ask her for the dance, The Waltz of the Toreadors, tra-la, take her by the waist and I say to myself—

how good I feel! What's happening to me! I have suddenly ceased to be afraid. It was an enchanted moment, Doctor.

DOCTOR. And did it happen again?

GENERAL. Every time. At all our pathetic little meetings. Each time came the miracle. I suddenly stopped being afraid.

DOCTOR. Why in heaven's name did you wait so long?

GENERAL. (*Sits Right desk chair.*) It's easy to talk. You don't know the old bitch—I mean my soul. When she is face to face with my wife, she bawls with disgust and fright; but when I make Emily cry, when she starts to whimper in her wheelchair—where I know she only sits in order to annoy me; when I am at last about to throttle her—don't laugh, it has crossed my mind—and take my cap off the hallstand to decamp once and for all; do you know what she does then, the great goop?— (my soul, that is). She cuts off my legs, she floods me with pity, mean ignoble pity, and old memories of love from the days when everything was not dried up and stale between us. She roots me to the spot. (*Rises— Crosses Up Left to above desk.*) So then I hang my cap back on the peg again and I take my soul on a little jaunt to the brothel to see if it won't cheer her up a bit. Have you got a soul, Doctor?

DOCTOR. Yes, but she's extremely shy and fairly modest in her demands.

GENERAL. (*Crosses to Right of* DOCTOR.) Well, don't let her get out of hand. Rule her with a rod of iron, for if you don't she'll have your skin! (*Crosses Left. Awed, stands by the door of the morning room. Murmuring dreamily.*) Dear Ghislaine! Dear sweet patient Ghislaine! Dear little soldier on half pay! Dear widow! (*Crosses Right and puts hand on* DOCTOR'S *shoulder.*) Give her a little less sedative than the other one, will you? I should so like to console her.

DOCTOR. (*Smiling.*) Very well. I am very fond of you, General. (*Pats his hand.*) And to think we were within an ace of murdering each other over that letter business!

GENERAL. (*Crosses Right below desk. Thumping his breast with clenched fist.*) God in heaven, what a fool I am! Suppose I thought of myself a little for a change! Me! Me! I exist too, don't I? (*Crosses to below sofa.*) Suppose I gave up trying to understand others for a minute? How good it would be! What do you say, Doctor?

DOCTOR. The best thing you could do, General, if you can bring yourself to do it.

GENERAL. Then it's all settled. Inspection over. (DOCTOR *rises.*) Dis-miss! Carry on!

SECRETARY. (*Enters at Up Center door.*) Good afternoon, Sir.

GENERAL. (*Crosses to him—pantomimes boxing.*) Ah there you are, my boy. You're in luck. I'm in a rollicking mood. (*Crosses to desk, takes out manuscript, puts on desk.*) We are going to mop up the chapter on Morocco in two shakes of a lamb's tail, and we'll postpone the next one until ten years from now. (SECRETARY *sits Right desk chair.*) I'll show them what stuff I'm made of!

DOCTOR. I'll leave you, General. (*Takes bag—crosses Up Right above* GENERAL.) My wife is going to think I'm here a bit too often. I don't have to tell you what reproaches are, eh? (*Shake hands—crosses Up Right Center.*) I shall look in to see them both this evening. You should take advantage of the sedative to rehearse your lines for the big scene.

GENERAL. I'm bearing them in mind. But it's so good to talk of something else for a minute. I shall take a little stroll around Morocco and come straight home again. (*The* DOCTOR *exits down the stairs.*) Now, let's get back to our two skypilots. As I was saying, there they were, with some parts missing. Write down: "A fearful mutilation, the details of which one hesitates to enlarge upon, perpetrated on the persons of two saintly churchmen, placed us under the sorry obligation of shedding blood ourselves."

(*Enter* ESTELLE *and* SIDONIA, *Up Center doors, followed*

by MME. DUPONT FREDAINE, *a mighty handsome dressmaker.*)

SIDONIA. (*Crosses Down Left Center near* SECRETARY.) Papa, we've come about the dresses.

GENERAL. Will you leave me in peace? I've other fish to fry just now. We go into the attack first thing in the morning.

MME. FREDAINE. (*Crosses to Center as girls clear Up Left a step.*) General!

GENERAL. (*Seeing her.*) Why, Mme. Dupont-Fredaine! (*Crosses to her—kisses her hand.*) I'm delighted to see you. (SECRETARY *rises, crosses Up Left above desk.*) Lovely and tempting and swish-swishing as ever! (*Swings her—circling Up Right of her—to below sofa.*) By Jove, what a figure! What allure! Mme. Dupont-Fredaine, you are the loveliest woman in the neighbourhood.

MME. FREDAINE. Now General, that's all over and done with. We must think of the young ones now. You gave us very little notice, you know—we had to perform miracles to make beauties out of these two girlies.

GENERAL. Miracles, how right you are. (*His foot taps hers.*)

MME. FREDAINE. (*Giving him a little slap.*) What do you say to this little frill at the bottom, (*Bends over to* ESTELLE'S *hem.*) hinted at again in the sleeves? I think it's a dream!

GENERAL. (*Crosses Up Center, pince-nez to his eyes; to her behind.*) Enchanting! Enchanting! Your own dress is delightful too. What is this splendid material? (*Crossing Down Right—touches back side.*)

MME. FREDAINE. (*Warding off the gesture.*) General! Look at your daughters. Their material is very much more beautiful.

GENERAL. (*Crosses Right below sofa. Vaguely.*) Lovely, lovely! Is it going to cost a lot?

MME. FREDAINE. (*Crosses Right to him.*) Now General, you know I'm very reasonable—

ACT II WALTZ OF THE TOREADORS 35

GENERAL. (*Close to her. Elbows her bosom.*) Oh, Emma, how I wish you were.

MME. FREDAINE. (*Crosses Up Left a step.*) Now, now. Let's not talk about the price. The young ladies wanted to make sure of pleasing you, and M. Gaston, too, I fancy!

SECRETARY. (*Flustered.*) But Madame, I am not qualified to judge. I have so little experience of young ladies.

MME. FREDAINE. (*Crosses Left a step.*) When one is twenty years of age and handsome, one is always qualified, young man. Why, he's blushing! He's adorable, this secretary of yours, General!

GENERAL. Ten thousand demons, Madam, I forbid you to adore him!

MME. FREDAINE. (*Crosses Down Right Center.*) Walk around the room will you, young ladies? The gentlemen will give us their verdict.

(*They circle Center then Up Left above and around desk—*ESTELLA *crosses to Left of* SECRETARY *and stops.* SIDONIA *stops Right of him.*)

GENERAL. (*Sotto voce to* MME. FREDAINE.) These repeated refusals are absurd, you know, Emma.

MME. FREDAINE. Stop it now. You are a wicked old wolf. My husband is a friend of yours.

GENERAL. Exactly. Nobody would take the least exception. (*She points to girls.*) Charming! Charming! I really must have a serious talk with you about the cost of these fal-lals, dear lady! Do come for a little stroll— (*Turns, takes her hand.*) around the garden, won't you? I shall present you with a rose. We won't be a moment, girls. Gaston, I leave them in your care, my boy. (*Goes out Up Center doors with* MME. FREDAINE. SECRETARY *crosses Right below* SIDONIA—*sits Right desk chair. The two* GIRLS *hurl themselves onto him.*)

SIDONIA. (*Crosses Left to him.*) Aren't you ashamed, letting her say you're adorable?

ESTELLE. (*Crosses Right to him above desk.*) An old flybynight like her! Doesn't it matter to you that we are pining away?

SECRETARY. But, my dear young ladies, how could I help it?

ESTELLE. And the other one this morning, I suppose you couldn't help her either? Why did you kiss her?

SIDONIA. It's shameful. Everybody saw you.

SECRETARY. I was alone. (*Rises, crosses Right Center.*)

ESTELLE. You don't think we ever leave you alone, do you? We never let you out of our sight. We were outside on the stairs.

SECRETARY. She had fallen on top of me. She was dying. What else could I do?

ESTELLE. (*Crosses to Right of him.*) You swore, Gaston.

SIDONIA. (*Crosses to Left of him.*) You swore. One or the other.

SECRETARY. I love you both, young ladies.

ESTELLE. Yet it's a third you kiss. A nice thing!

SIDONIA. (*Crosses Down Left to Right desk chair.*) Ah, my dear—men! Does it surprise you? What a little child you are!

ESTELLE. You never even kiss us!

SECRETARY. But you are young ladies. Besides there are always two of you.

SIDONIA. (*Crosses Right to Left of him.*) Ooh!

ESTELLE *and* SIDONIA. (*Turn to each other in fury.*) You see!

ESTELLE. You never let me see him alone!

SIDONIA. No, it's you!

ESTELLE. 'T'isn't! It's you!

SIDONIA. 'T'isn't! It's you! You pudding!

ESTELLE. You skinny lizard!

SIDONIA. You old bag of lard! You soppy sausage you!

ESTELLE. You string bean! (*They fight. The* SECRETARY *distracted, hops ineffectually around trying to separate them.* SIDONIA *pulls off* ESTELLE'S *belt, chases her Up Left with it—around desk and Down Right—*

back to Center. ESTELLE *pulls* SIDONIA'S *sleeve out.* SIDONIA *throws belt on floor, runs to Right window— then to Up Center door.*)

SECRETARY. Ladies! Ladies! Help! Help! Oh my goodness, they'll murder each other!

(MME. DUPONT-FREDAINE *and the* GENERAL, *very red in the face, come flying in.*)

MME. FREDAINE. (*Separates them.* SIDONIA *swings around to start again.* SIDONIA *Left,* ESTELLA *Right.*) Young ladies! Your dresses! (SECRETARY *runs Right above sofa to Down Right.*)

GENERAL. (*Shouting, crosses Down Center.*) Holy suffering catfish, have you finished? (*They stop.*) Where did I get such a pair of misbegotten frumps?! What is going on? Explain yourselves!

SIDONIA. (*At Right desk chair.*) She started it!

ESTELLE. (*At Left end of sofa.*) I didn't! She did!

GENERAL. (*Crosses Right to* SECRETARY.) Devil take it, man, I leave them in your charge and you can't even stop them fighting!

MME. FREDAINE. (*Down Right Center. On her knees repairing the damage.*) Oh, your dresses! Your dresses! Little vandals!

GENERAL. Answer me! What were they fighting about?

SECRETARY. (*Crimson.*) I can't tell you, Sir.

GENERAL. Can't tell me, eh? (*Turns Left a step.*) Ye Gods and little fishes, who is making a monkey out of who? You two, come here! What were you fighting about? (*No answer. They cross to Down Center.*)

ESTELLE. (*Blurting it out.*) Papa! We love him to distraction!

SIDONIA. Both of us!

GENERAL. Whom?

ESTELLE *and* SIDONIA. (*Sobbing and pointing to* SECRETARY.) Him!

GENERAL. (*Turns Right.*) That is the rampaging limit!

ESTELLE. But Papa, you don't know what it's like to

be in love! (*Kneels on sofa—face buried.* SIDONIA *sits Right desk chair.*)

MME. FREDAINE. (*Behind her—trying to stop her.*) Ladies! Ladies! You're weeping onto your dresses!

GENERAL. (*Crosses Up Center. Turns front.*) Blood and giblets, that's a good one! That emasculated virgin?

MME. FREDAINE. (*Covers* SIDONIA'S *ears.*) General!

GENERAL. Sorry, it slipped out. That zany? That trashy little penpusher?

ESTELLE. (*Lifts head.*) Papa, what's emasculated?

GENERAL. Jumping Jehosophat, leave the room this instant! (*They go Up Center.*) Be so good as to take them away, Mme. Dupont-Fredaine, and leave me with this young bumpkin here. I don't know what's going on in this house but things are beginning to get out of hand. (*Crosses Up Right Center.*)

MME. FREDAINE. (*Crosses Right Center to* GENERAL.) It's love, General!

GENERAL. That's rich! Love isn't an excuse for everything.

MME. FREDAINE. (*Giving him a surreptitious little slap on her way out.*) Naughty fibber, you. You just told me the very opposite! Goodbye for the moment. (*Crosses up to platform. Turns front.*)

GENERAL. (*Winking.*) See you later, Emma. (*The* WOMEN *go out. Crosses Down Center.*) Well, what have you got to say for yourself, sir?

SECRETARY. (*Steps Left below sofa.*) I don't know, sir. I am quite overcome.

GENERAL. (*Center.*) Exactly! You were recommended to me by a venerable ecclesiastic who vouched for your morals and your handwriting. I had up till now testified to the excellence of both.

SECRETARY. I swear to you that nothing in my behavior could have incited the young ladies to—

GENERAL. (*Turns away.*) Don't drown the salmon, sir! (*Turns to him.*) Nothing in your behavior could have incited you to kiss Mlle. de Ste-Euverte on the mouth this morning either, I suppose? (*Points to sofa.*)

SECRETARY. She mistook me for someone else, sir.

GENERAL. That makes it even worse! You are an impostor, sir!

SECRETARY. No, General, the terrifying thing is that while I held her in my arms I quite thought for a moment that it was me she loved.

GENERAL. She wasn't properly conscious, my boy.

SECRETARY. (*Bitterly.*) She kept calling me Leon.

GENERAL. (*Easily.*) Leon? What a coincidence! (*Crosses Left below desk.*) The name of her intended, no doubt?

SECRETARY. But all the same it was to me she said it.

GENERAL. (*Bursting out laughing.*) Ha ha, that's a good one! That's very good! (*Turns to him.*) So you think one falls in love like that, do you? At first sight and for always? Fiddlesticks! You must gorge yourself on cheap novels. (*Sits Down Right corner of desk.*)

SECRETARY. No sir, on the classics, exclusively. But the course of events is frequently quite similar. (*With dignity.*) In any case I intend to confess to this lady when she is once more herself, and offer to make amends.

GENERAL. Confess? Confess what? You will do not such thing. I will not have you confuse the wits of this unfortunate girl. (*Crosses Right to him.*) Am I going to have to teach you, by roundly boxing your ears, just what a young girl's honour means? I've seen you already, my lad, with that last little maid we had here. (SECRETARY *gestures.*) Don't deny it. I tell you I saw you!

SECRETARY. It was *she* who pursued me, sir. I avoided her, she was always coming up behind me in the passages—

GENERAL. (*Sits Right desk chair.*) Oh, the little bitch!

SECRETARY. She said she was fed to the teeth with this dump—(GENERAL *turns.*) I quote of course—and that she absolutely had to have a young one.

GENERAL. (*Interrupting in a voice of thunder.*) Young man! You are on the threshold of life. You appear to me to be completely devoid of principles. (*Rises.*) You were put into my care—I could be your father—(*Paces Up*

Center.) and it is my duty to instil those principles into you. (SECRETARY *starts to speak.*) Hold your tongue! You will speak when your turn comes and not before. Sit down! (SECRETARY *sits Right desk chair.*) Firstly, (*Crosses Down Right Center.*) one point about which it is forbidden to make light. Honor. Do you know what I mean by honor?

SECRETARY. Yes, sir.

GENERAL. (*Pacing Center.*) I should hope so. You have been bred on the classics you say? I do not therefore have to teach you the fable of that Spartan youth who, having stolen a fox and hidden it beneath his tunic, preferred to have his stomach gnawed away sooner than confess his theft? This admirable fable contains a moral. Will you kindly tell me what that moral is?

SECRETARY. (*After a moment's hesitation.*) Never confess.

GENERAL. (*Standing Right Center.*) No sir, wrong answer.

SECRETARY. Never steal a fox?

GENERAL. Wrong again. He did steal. But having stolen, what remained for our young Spartan to do then?

SECRETARY. Give back the fox and take his punishment.

GENERAL. No, sir. In allowing his stomach to be gnawed away without a murmur he did better. He showed that he had honor. Draw the moral, now that I have put you on the right track.

SECRETARY. When one does something contrary to honor, honor consists in never owning up to it.

GENERAL. No, sir! That is pride, which is an insufferable fault.

SECRETARY. I give up, sir.

GENERAL. (*Steps back.*) Ha! You give up do you? Do you indeed? I can see your sense of honor is choking you! A nice bunch, I must say, the younger generation! If the War Office is counting on your sort to hoist the flag . . . (*Crosses Up Right and circles above sofa. Back to Right Center.*) However, the meaning of this

ACT II WALTZ OF THE TOREADORS

fable sir, is very simple. Honor bids me not to steal. Right, I do steal—unless one is a born idiot, one sidesteps the rules and regulations now and then. But one thing is certain; I am not capable of forfeiting my honor. Therein lies the principle. I have been caught. Therein lies the accident. Never let yourself be caught. Am I, a young Spartan going to be found wanting in honor? No. I cannot be found wanting in honor. Hence there is no fox under my tunic. You get it?

SECRETARY. No, sir.

GENERAL. (*Crosses Up Center.*) Never mind. You'll understand when you grow up. Simply retain from all this that it is essential to keep up appearances. Let us take a more familiar instance. (*Sits desk chair.*) You are sleeping with the maid.

SECRETARY. (*Shocked.*) General!

GENERAL. Don't have a fit. You were on the verge of doing so, you young pecksniff. And if you weren't a born ass you would have. To resume, honor is strong, but the flesh is weak. You are hot-blooded. You've got the wench under your skin. When she brushes past you in the passage, something goes "BMMF" in your stomach. Do you for all that pinch her bottom at table in the middle of luncheon?

SECRETARY. (*Blushing at the suggestion.*) Oh no, sir.

GENERAL. No, you simply say, "Leontine, please bring us some bread." And yet you know perfectly well it isn't a bread roll you're after. Luncheon runs its course, impeccably. Does it not?

SECRETARY. Yes sir.

GENERAL. Life, Gaston, is one long family lunch, tiresome because it has to be performed—according to a long established ritual, with initialed napkin rings, embroidered table mats, forks of different shapes and sizes and a bell push under the table. It is a game we have agreed to play. So we must play it according to the rules; answer the children's questions, divide the plum tart into equal slices, scold the youngest when he dribbles, fold one's napkin nicely and put it back into its ring—until the coffee. But the coffee once drunk, down the back stairs and the best of luck. The law of the jungle comes into its own. Dammit, there's no need to be a complete fool. (SECRETARY *starts to speak*.) Quiet! I haven't finished. I can see the way your mind's working. You are young, you want the moon—you are going to say— "That's middle class hypocrisy— What about ideals? Where does the ideal come in?"

SECRETARY. Yes, sir.

GENERAL. Well, my boy, the ideal is doing very nicely, thank you. The ideal, my friend, is the lifebuoy. You're in the ocean, splashing about, doing your damndest not to drown. You can try to swim in the right direction in spite of the whirlpools and cross currents; the main thing is to do the regulation breast-stroke and if you're not a clod, never to let the buoy out of your sight. No one expects any more than that of you. Now if you relieve yourself in the water now and then, that's your affair. The sea is big, and if the top half of your body still looks as though it's doing the regulation breast-stroke, nobody will say a word.

SECRETARY. But does one never reach the lifebuoy, General?

GENERAL. Never. But if your heart's in the right place, you never lose sight of it either. These few fanatics who try a faster stroke to reach it at all costs, deluge everybody else and always finish up by drowning, generally dragging God knows how many poor devils under with them, who could otherwise have gone on quietly floundering about and minding their own business. Do you see what I mean?

SECRETARY. No, sir. Might I say something though?

GENERAL. Go ahead, my boy. Your turn to speak now.

SECRETARY. I am twenty years old, General. I would rather try to go fast and drown.

GENERAL. (*Starts to scold—stops. Gently, after a pause*.) You are right, my boy. It's a sorry business, growing old, and understanding. Lieutenant St. Pe! Graduated second from Saumur! Volunteer! Wait for me! I'm done for anyway—here goes, I'd rather drown! I only said all that because one has to. Try all the same not to drown others, even in a good cause. That's what weighs heavy on a man, hurting other people. I have got used to everything, but not to that.

GENERAL'S WIFE. (*Off.*) Leon!

GENERAL. Yes!

GENERAL'S WIFE. Leon, where are you?

GENERAL. (*Wearily.*) I'm here! I'm here, for Heaven's sake! I'm always here.

GENERAL'S WIFE. (*Off.*) Come and sit with me, Leon. Goodness only knows what you're playing at while you think I'm asleep.

GENERAL. (*Looking at the* SECRETARY *with a smile. Rises.*) Playing the fool, my dear, with a young spark who wasn't even listening and quite right he was too, damn him! (*Slapping him on the back—crosses to Right Center.*) Wait a bit, my boy. There's no almighty hurry after all, even if they do make fun of you. Wait until the right girl comes along and with her you will miraculously cease to be afraid. But when you find her, by Hades don't wait seventeen years!

SECRETARY. I won't, sir. (*Rises, Left of* GENERAL.)

GENERAL. At once! Remember my advice! Immediately! And make for the lifebuoy, side by side. (*Crosses and puts hand on* SECRETARY'S *shoulder.*) The only proper way to swim is two by two. Wish me luck. I'm going in myself. But it's on the cards that one of us may drown en route.

WIFE. (*Off.*) Leon!

GENERAL. Here I am, Madam. At your service for the last time. (*Goes into her room.*)

SECRETARY. (*Crosses Up Center—looks at bedroom door—then Left door.*) At once! That's all I'll keep of his advice! (*Takes his courage in both hands and goes into the morning room.* GHISLAINE *is heard murmuring through the open door.*)

GHISLAINE. Leon! Leon, you've come back! Can it be true then? Will I really never be alone again? Oh, Leon!

SECRETARY. (*A pause. Re-enters, crosses to Center, dazed and staggering a little.*) The lady is still making a mistake. And yet, despite the action of the sedative, something tells me that she isn't altogether taken in. How interesting it is, living! The Reverend Fathers never told me. (*He screws up his courage and goes back into the room.*)

CURTAIN

ACT TWO

Scene 2

SCENE: *The same, except that the wall which hid the General's Wife's room from view has been removed. It is afternoon. The shutters have been closed in the General's room now deserted, as well as in the other. The* GENERAL'S WIFE, *in night cap and bedjacket, is sitting up among her pillows in her monumental quilted bed. The* GENERAL *is standing.*

GENERAL. (*Paces Left of Left chair.*) We must thrash this matter out, Madam, once and for all.

WIFE. I tried to kill myself, you monster, isn't that enough for you?

GENERAL. (*Down Left.*) You were stretched out on the tracks—an awkward position but quite safe. The train had already passed.

WIFE. I didn't know! I was waiting for it!

GENERAL. On that branch line you could reckon on a good twenty-four hours of it.

WIFE. Is nothing sacred to you? You brute! I might have died of cold during the night!

GENERAL. We are well into April, and spring was early this year. We are dying of heat.

ACT II WALTZ OF THE TOREADORS 45

WIFE. Of sunstroke then—starvation, I don't know.
. . . Of sorrow—yes, that's it—quite simply of sorrow,
in my state of health.

GENERAL. Sorrow you can die of in your bed, Madam,
at leisure. It was absurd, like everything else you do.

WIFE. I am seriously ill. How often has the doctor told
you that my condition gives cause for the gravest alarm?
I did truly mean to kill myself and that alone should
make you fall sobbing at my feet, if your heart were not
made of granite!

GENERAL. My heart is not made of granite, Madam,
but I am thrifty with my tears.

WIFE. I sacrificed my life for you! (*Screaming.*) Murderer!

GENERAL. Be quiet, confound you, or I'll leave the
room! Let us talk things over calmly. (*Sits chair Left
of bed.*)

WIFE. I'm too unhappy. You aren't unhappy, not you.
You have your health and strength, you have. You're up
and dressed each morning, you ride your horse, you walk
around the garden, you go drinking with your friends.
You live! You jeer at me, on your two legs, while I sit
glued to my wheelchair. Aren't you ashamed of being
well? (*Gets pill.*)

GENERAL. You are glued to your wheelchair for no
other reason than because you want to be. We know that
now.

WIFE. (*Takes pill—drinks water.*) Do you dare to say
that I'm not ill?

GENERAL. One has to be an idiot like myself, Madam,
to go on believing in your aches and pains by this time.
As for your poor ailing legs, thank God we'll hear no
more about those for a bit. I strongly suspect you of
stretching them in your room every night. They helped
you keep your balance mighty well down the wistaria and
over to the railway line this morning.

WIFE. It was the last spasm of the stricken beast who
longs for death! Call your accomplice, Doctor Bonfant,
with his rubber mallet; let him test my reflexes.

GENERAL. Death and damnation, Madam, that's too easy!

WIFE. Too easy for you, I daresay. What have you got to complain about? While I lie here, racked with pain, you who can wander fancy free on your great fat legs, where do you go, eh?

GENERAL. From my study to the garden, at your beck and call every ten minutes.

WIFE. And what is there in the garden? Answer me that, you pig, you satyr, you lascivious goat!

GENERAL. Well, I dunno . . . roses . . .

WIFE. (*Cackling*.) Roses! There's Madame Tardieu on the other side of the privet hedges. That frightful woman who exhibits her bodice as she leans over her flower beds. Yes they're a household word hereabouts, Madame Tardieu's breasts! Whalebone, rubber, steel probably—she's propped up like a tumbledown barn.

GENERAL. All right, all right, all right! After all, I haven't been to look.

WIFE. You dream of nothing else. You'll be mighty disillusioned when the great day comes. But on the other side of the fence at the bottom of the garden, walking along the school path at midday and at four, there are younger ones, aren't there? (*Turns away*.) The little convent girls! You centaur! One of these days the parents will complain.

GENERAL. You're wandering, Madam. They say goodmorning to me, and I say goodmorning back.

WIFE. And what about Prize Giving Day, at which you always manage to officiate, you old faun!—When you kiss them, red as a lobster in your uniform?

GENERAL. It's the custom.

WIFE. What you're thinking isn't the custom and you know it! You tickle their bosoms with your decorations as you lean over them. Don't say you don't. I've seen you.

GENERAL. If nothing worse happens to them as they're growing up we'll make mayqueens out of them!

WIFE. Queens of the May indeed! You've always been

ACT II   WALTZ OF THE TOREADORS   47

ready to officiate on May Day too. Last year's one, that hussy, as you kissed her, you whispered something in her ear. It was reported to me.

GENERAL. (*Chaffingly.*) I whispered something? You don't say so?

WIFE. You arranged to meet her, I know. Besides I've seen her since. She's pregnant.

GENERAL. Nonsense, she's putting on weight, that's all.

WIFE. My maids are putting on weight *too*, one after another.

GENERAL. (*Rises, crosses Down Left.*) Let's change the subject, Madam. I have something very serious to say to you. (*Crosses up to Left of bed.*) You are untrue to me, Madam, that's the long and short of it. You wrote to Dr. Bonfant that you were in love with him. I have proof of it here in my wallet, down in black and white with two spelling mistakes which identify your hand. Yes, for you have always accused me of being a clodhopper, too lumpish to appreciate Baudelaire or Wagner, but you can't tell a conjunction from a carrot. You never had a day's schooling in your life.

WIFE. How shabby you are! To come to my deathbed and throw my unhappy childhood in my face! For over a year I was a boarder with the daughters of consuls and ambassadors in the most select ladies' college in Paris.

GENERAL. Where your mother went to do the household mending and where they took you in and fed you out of charity.

WIFE. My poor mother and I suffered a great deal, no doubt. But please to remember that my mother was a woman of infinite distinction, not a little provincial housewife like yours.

GENERAL. One trade is as good as another, but your mother, Madam, was a dresser at the Opera.

WIFE. She accepted the post at the earnest request of the Director, solely for love of music.

GENERAL. (*Crosses Up to Left of bed.*) Have it your own way. Let us get back to those letters. Did you or did you not write them? Do you or do you not address him as "Armand"? Do you tell him, yes or no, that his hair smells of vanilla when he sounds your chest, and that you pretend to have a belly ache so he can come and feel it for you? It's down in black and white with two spelling mistakes, in your own handwriting.

WIFE. How could you stoop so low as to come poking about in my correspondence?

GENERAL. I did not poke about in your correspondence, Madam. I obtained possession of those letters. How? That's none of your business.

WIFE. Oh isn't it? None of my business? (GENERAL *turns away Left.*) Those letters were in the drawer of my bedside table where I keep my curlers and other objects of an intimate nature. You tell me they are in your wallet. And you dare to cross-question *me?* It's past belief! I did think you were still a gentleman.

GENERAL. (*Turns to her.*) Dammit, Madam, will you stick to the point?

WIFE. So you ransack a lady's drawers, do you, my lad? You try to dishonor her, you a senior officer? All right then, I shall tell. I shall tell everybody. I shall get up, I'll recover, for a day, the use of my poor aching legs, and the night of the reception at the annual Tattoo, in front of all the high ranking military personnel, I shall make a sensational entrance and I shall tell all!

GENERAL. (*Turns to her.*) I repeat I have not ransacked your drawers.

WIFE. Have you those letters?

GENERAL. (*Crosses Down.*) I have.

WIFE. Show them to me.

GENERAL. (*Sits Left chair, puts it downstage.*) Ha ha! Not on your life.

WIFE. Very well. If you really have those letters in your wallet, there can be nothing more between us, but an ocean of contempt. You may go. I am sleepy, I'm asleep. (*She lies with her eyes closed.*)

GENERAL. No, Madam, you are not asleep. That would be too easy. Open your eyes. Open your eyes, this instant, do you hear, or I'll open them for you! (*Rises, crosses to her.*) Emily! Do as I say! Open your eyes. (*He shakes her, slaps her, forces her eyelids up from their white eyeballs, begins to lose his head.*) Come to your senses, damn you! What new game are you playing now?

WIFE. (*Sits up straight. Weakly.*) My heart.

GENERAL. What about your heart!

WIFE. It's shrinking. Goodbye, Leon! (*Takes his arm.*) I never loved anyone else but you. (*Gasps and sinks back.*)

GENERAL. (*Back a step.*) Oh no, not your heart attack. We haven't even raised our voices. Your heart attack is for after the big scenes, Madam. You are warm, your pulse is good. I'm not falling for that. (*Shaking her.*) Wake up! Emily! (*Pulls her up.*) You can't be as rigid as that. You're doing it on purpose. (*Lets her go— She falls back.*) I'll give you your drops. (*He rummages about among the bottles on the side table Left of bed— then Down Left cabinet.*) Holy Moses, what a collection! It would take a qualified druggist to make head or tail of this lot! There's enough here to upset the constitution of a cart horse. Needless to say, no dropper. Where the devil did Eugenie put the thing? (*Rummages, holds up bottle. Locks both doors.*) Oh well here goes—one drop more—one drop less the way things are now . . . (*Stirs with fingers.*) There Emily, drink this, and if that doesn't do the trick I'll call the doctor. Unclench your teeth, my love. (*Puts it to her lips—tries to open mouth.*) Unclench your teeth damn you, it's dripping all over you! Give me strength— (*Puts glass down and crosses to Down Left cabinet—down on one knee.*) What's the matter with you? Your pulse is all right. There's no getting away from that. I'll give you your injection.

WIFE. (*Feebly.*) You're still rummaging, Leon. You're suspicious of me even on my deathbed.

GENERAL. (*Straightens—half turns.*) I'm *not* rummaging, I'm looking for your capsules.

WIFE. (*Flops on Right side.*) Too late. Call the children.

GENERAL. (*Crosses to bed—straightens her knees on stool.*) What are you raving about, my dear?—you aren't going to die. You're weak, that's all. I'll get the doctor. (*Starts—She pulls him back—He lands sprawling on stool.*)

WIFE. Too late. I implore you, don't move, Leon. Stay with me. Hold my hand as you did in the old days, long ago, when I was ill. You took care of me then, you were patient with me. You used to bathe my temples with eau de cologne and murmur sweet nothings in my ear . . .

GENERAL. (*Left of table. Looking for the bottle and mumbling.*) I can still dab you with a bit of cologne . . . (*Pours on handkerchief.*)

WIFE. But without the sweet nothings! It's that that's killing me—you murderer!

GENERAL. (*Not seeing—puts in her mouth then quickly to her head.*) There. That will revive you.

WIFE. (*Leaves hankie on head.*) It frightens you, eh, to hear me say it? I'm dying for want of your love, Leon!

GENERAL. (*On knees.*) No, no, no, don't be silly now. To begin with you are not dying at all, and you know perfectly well, my love, that I am always full of attention for you. (*Tucks blanket.*)

WIFE. (*Throws hankie to wall.*) Attentions! What do I want with your attentions! (*Grabs his arms.*) I want you to love me, Leon, as you used to long ago, when you took me in your arms and called me your little girl, when you bit me all over. . . . Aren't I your little girl any more, to be carried naked to my bath? (*Tips his face up—looks into it.*)

GENERAL. (*Uncomfortably.*) Emily, we all have to grow up sometime. (*Struggling to get away.*)

WIFE. (*Plaintively.*) Why don't you bite me all over like a young terrier any more?

GENERAL. (*More and more embarrassed.*) Dammit, Madam, young terriers grow into old ones—(*Rises and turns Left.*) after twenty years. Besides, I've lost my teeth. (*Sinks into Left chair.*)

WIFE. (*Sitting up with astonishing vigour considering her heart attack.*) You've teeth enough for others, you mealy-mouthed old fraud! You can talk about those letters which were never even sent. I have evidence of another sort, in a trinket box underneath my mattress, letters both sent and received, where there's no question of your having lost your teeth. Letters in which you play the young man for another's benefit—and there you flatter yourself incidentally, my poor Leon—for apart from your summary prowess with the maids, you needn't think you're capable of much in that line either—

GENERAL. (*Rises, crosses Left to window.*) Be quiet, Madam! What do you know about it?

WIFE. I know as much as all women left unsatisfied. Learn first to satisfy one woman, to be a man in her bed, before you go scampering into the beds of others.

GENERAL. (*Turns Right to her.*) So I have never been a man in your bed, Madam, is that it?

WIFE. Soon weary, my friend, soon asleep, and when for a wonder you had a little energy, soon replete. We would both close our eyes in the bed, but while you performed your little task picturing the Lord knows whom, you don't imagine do you, that it was you I thought about?

GENERAL. (*Turns away Left.*) How vulgar you are, Madam—vulgar and shameless. However, if that was so, why the reproaches and the scenes, why so many tears for so long?

WIFE. Because you belong to me, Leon! You are mine like my house, mine like my jewels, mine like my furniture, mine like your name. (*Starts kneeling.*)

GENERAL. And is that what you understand by love?

WIFE. (*In a great and frightful cry, standing on her bed in her nightshirt, a nightmarish figure.*) Yes!

GENERAL. (*Crosses to foot of bed.*) Death and damnation, Madam, I do not belong to you!

WIFE. To whom then?

GENERAL. (*Crosses to below Right end of bed.*) To no one. To myself perhaps.

WIFE. No! Not any longer. I am your wife. Your wife before God and before the law.

GENERAL. Hells bells, Madam, I'll escape you!

WIFE. Never!

GENERAL. I'll pretend not to know you.

WIFE. I'll scream, I'll cause a riot! I'll break things. I'll run up debts to ruin you—

GENERAL. (*Crosses to below Center, Right of bed.*) I tell you I'll take a train and disappear into thin air. You won't know where I am.

WIFE. You'd never dare, and if you did, I'd follow you to the far ends of the earth!

GENERAL. (*Turns to her, Left corner of bed.*) And when I die, hell's teeth! Will you make that journey too?

WIFE. When you die, I shall cry out loud—"I was his wife!" I shall put on widow's weeds, I, and I alone, will have the right and I shall visit your grave on All Souls' Day. I'll have my name engraved on your tombstone and when my turn comes to die I shall come and lie beside you for eternity. Unknown people as they pass will still read that I was your wife, on the stone!

GENERAL. (*Crosses to Down Left corner of bed.*) By God, I hate you, Madam.

WIFE. (*Leans forward.*) What difference does that make? I am your wife.

GENERAL. (*Crosses to Left of her.*) I hate the sight and sound of you! And I'll tell you something else that's stronger even than my hatred and disgust. I am dying of boredom, Madam, by your side.

WIFE. You bore me too, but I am your wife just the same and about that you can do nothing.

GENERAL. (*Crosses Down Left.*) But devil take it, you hate me just as much!

WIFE. Yes, I hate you. You ruined my career. I had a superb voice, a dazzling future—you insisted that I give up the stage. All that was brilliant in me you crushed underfoot. Other men worshipped me; you frightened them away with your great sword. You created a desert around me with your stupid jealousy, you made me unlearn how to be beautiful—unlearn how to love and be loved. Expected me to keep house for you like a servant, to feed your sickly children, I, whose breasts were famous throughout Paris!

GENERAL. (*Down Left.*) Your breasts famous? Don't make me laugh. Where did you exhibit them anyway? In Lohengrin?

WIFE. At festivals of Art. Before people whose refinement and luxurious living your petty tradesman's world can't even guess at. (*Gets back down in bed—leans back on head board.*) Have you ever thought, you desperado, of all I sacrificed for you?

GENERAL. Death and damnation, (*Paces to Right and then Left.*) Madam, that is ancient history! I am resolved to sue for a divorce. (*Left of foot of bed.*)

WIFE. A divorce! You could never live alone, you're far too frightened. And who do you think would have you, you poor devil?

GENERAL. I've found someone who will have me.

WIFE. She must be very old and pretty ugly—or pretty poor to be reduced to that.

GENERAL. It's a lie. She is young and beautiful. She's true to me. She is waiting for me.

WIFE. Since when?

GENERAL. Since—since seventeen years.

WIFE. You must be joking, my dear. Seventeen years! And you think she loves you? And you think you love her? And they've been waiting seventeen years, poor lambs!

GENERAL. (*Sits Left chair.*) Yes Madam, and because of you.

WIFE. Oh Leon, if I weren't so ill, I'd laugh! I'd laugh like a mad thing! It's too silly—really too silly! Seventeen years! But if you really loved her, you poor imbecile, you would have left me long ago!

GENERAL. I stayed out of respect for your grief and

pity for your illness, which I long took to be genuine, Madam.

WIFE. What a fool you are! Do you think I couldn't dance if I wanted to? (*She gets out of bed—Right side.*) Look! You see how well I can stand! Come and dance with me. Come! (*Crosses Down and Left to him. She sings and dances a few steps.*)

GENERAL. Let me go! You're mad! Go back to bed.

WIFE. (*Tries to pull him Right.*) No. You are my true love and I want to dance with you. Like at the Ball at the Military College in Saumur, the one of '93, seventeen years ago funnily enough. (*Stops dancing—below bed.*) Do you remember?

GENERAL. Confound you, why?

WIFE. Because you were so handsome and scintillating and sure of yourself with the women at that Ball. "Major St. Pé!" How smartly you clicked your heels, German fashion, when you introduced yourself! How fetchingly you smoothed your whiskers, how prettily you kissed their hands! (*Sits foot of bed.*) I shall never forget that ball. I was still in love with you then, and I had stayed faithful, idiot that I was, in spite of your lady friends whom you forced me to invite to dinner. But at that ball I suddenly had enough, all at once, in the space of a second. You were dancing a waltz with a ninny of a girl —I saw you whisper in her ear and she made eyes at you and simpered. The Waltz of the Toreadors—I even remember the tune. (*She sings.*) I was too wretched. I had to get away, out of the ballroom. I went out into the hall to order my carriage. There was a man there, younger and handsomer than you, and he helped me. And when he found our carriage he said I couldn't possibly go home alone and he climbed in to escort me.

GENERAL. Well?

WIFE. Well, you were still waltzing, my poor dear, with your superb half turns and your airs and graces. What do you suppose women are made of? He became my lover.

GENERAL. What? You have had a lover, Madam, and

it was at that Saumur ball that you made his acquaintance? A man who had merely helped you find our carriage, a complete stranger?—I won't even ask you his rank. How horrible! But I'd like to believe that you had a few doubts, dear God!—a few misgivings, before taking such a step. I fondly hope you did at least wait a little?

WIFE. Of course, my dear. I was a respectable woman. I waited.

GENERAL. How long?

WIFE. Three days.

GENERAL. (*Exploding.*) Holy suffering rattlesnakes! (*Rises, crosses Down Left to window.*) I waited seventeen years, Madam, and I'm waiting still!

WIFE. (*Rises, crosses to Right of bed—leans over.*) And when that one was posted, I forget where, to the devil—to the Far East, I took another just as handsome, and another, and again another, and so on before I grew too old and there would only be you left who would have me.

GENERAL. (*Turns to her.*) But dammit, if you were untrue to me why the tears and the reproaches—why the immense heartaches and the torment—why this illness?

WIFE. To keep you, Leon. To keep you for always because I am your wife. For I do love you, Leon, on top of everything. I hate you for all the harm you did to me, but I love you—not tenderly, you fool, not with seventeen years of waiting and letter-writing, (*Climbs on bed and stands.*) not for the bliss of being in your arms at night—we have never made love together, you poor wretch, and you know it—not for your conversation— you bore me—not for your rank either, nor your money —I've been offered more—I love you because you are mine, my object, my thing, my hold-all, my garbage bin—

GENERAL. No! (*Turns Down Left.*)

WIFE. Yes, and you know it! And whatever you may promise others you know you will never be anything but that.

GENERAL. (*Wildly.*) No!

WIFE. Yes! You will never be able to bring yourself to hurt me, you're too cowardly. You know it, and you know I know it, too.

GENERAL. No! (*Crosses Left to Down Left corner.*)

WIFE. (*Gets off Left side.*) Yes! Come now, darling, dance with me. The Waltz of the Toreadors, the last waltz, with me this time. (*Crosses to him, arms out.*)

GENERAL. No! (*Pushes her away.*)

WIFE. (*Backs off Right—below bed.*) Yes! I want you to. And you want whatever I want. Come, dance with your chronic invalid, your old bag of bones. Come dance with your remorse! Come dance with your love!

GENERAL. (*Backs up Left.*) Don't touch me, for pity's sake, don't touch me! (*She pursues him. He cringes in a corner. All of a sudden he stretches out his arms, grips her throat and yells—forces her back on bed, her head flopping over foot—body Upstage.*) Phantasmagoria!! (*The* GENERAL'S WIFE *struggles in her voluminous nightgown, trying to tear his hands away from her throat.*)

CURTAIN

ACT THREE

SCENE: *When the LIGHTS go up, the wall of the General's Wife's room is back in place. The GENERAL is alone in his study. It is evening. He prowls about like a caged bear, a shadow in the gathering darkness. All of a sudden he stops and cries out. The SOUND of a BUGLE is heard. He gets binoculars from scrim wall and peers out window as the DOCTOR comes out of* MME. ST. PÉ's *room. The GENERAL looks at him in silence.*

DOCTOR. I have just taken her blood pressure. She's as right as rain. She had a bad fright, that's all. (*Puts bag down by bedroom door.*)

GENERAL. (*Leaves binoculars on window sill and sits Down Right.*) So did I.

DOCTOR. (*Crossing Down Right.*) So did I, my friend. The moment your maid appeared and said to come at once, Madam was choking, I guessed.

GENERAL. What did she say?

DOCTOR. Who? Your maid?

GENERAL. My wife.

DOCTOR. (*Sits Right end of sofa.*) My poor friend, she seems to think it quite in order that you should want to do away with her. Murder is the regular concomitant of passion at the opera. She submits gracefully, biding her time no doubt, and feeling vaguely flattered: she is more than ever convinced that you are a pair of sublime and star crossed lovers.

GENERAL. Oh, the idiocy of it! Will she never understand that she quite simply bores me?

DOCTOR. I'm afraid you will have to face up to it, General. Never.

GENERAL. But dear God, that can't be all there is to life! Why did no one ever warn me? Everybody looks happy round about me, and content. How do they do it, damn them—how do they manage not to suffer? What is their password? Let them tell it me, at once. I've no more time to wait.

DOCTOR. My dear old friend, I think that is a question one must ask oneself when one is very much younger.

GENERAL. (*Rises, yelling.*) I *am* young! Lieutenant St. Pé! (*Crosses to Right Center.*) I decline all other rank! It's nothing but a booby-trap! I see it now. (*Suddenly.*) Doctor, has medicine not discovered anything to put the clock back seventeen years?

DOCTOR. Nothing so far.

GENERAL. Are you sure?

DOCTOR. It would surely have been mentioned in certain . . . specialist publications.

GENERAL. (*Crosses Right to Down Right window.*) I'm in no mood for levity. Are you aware what's going on? Mademoiselle de Ste-Euverte and my secretary have gone out for a walk. They've been away nearly two hours.

DOCTOR. Nothing very odd about that. You were closeted with your wife; your explanations bode fair to going on forever. I expect they simply decided to go for a short stroll while they were waiting.

GENERAL. (*Turns to* DOCTOR.) A curious misunderstanding arose between the two of them this morning. They left, with their little fingers linked, so the maid tells me. Does that strike you as normal too? (*Crosses Left above sofa to Down Center.*) As for my daughters, who were enamoured of our hero—they have gone as well, leaving this letter on the table, together with their fake jewelry wrapped up in tissue paper. (*He pulls a letter out of his pocket.*) "We are too unhappy. He is in love with another. We prefer to die—" (two more of them, it's all the rage in this house.)—"tell Madame Dupont-Fredaine not to go on with our dresses." Among other primordial virtues, their mother has imbued them with a solid notion of economy.

DOCTOR. Good Heavens, and haven't they come home yet?

GENERAL. I sent the gardener in search of them. They

ACT III WALTZ OF THE TOREADORS 59

must be down by the pond, dabbling their feet in the water. They are far too plain to kill themselves. Everything is tumbling about my ears! Dear God, how will it all end? (*Crosses Left—sit Right desk chair.*)

DOCTOR. As in real life, or in the theatre, in the days when plays *were* plays—a contrived denouement, not too gloomy on the face of it, and which doesn't really fool a soul, and then a little later—curtain. (*Rises, crosses Right to Down Right chair.*) I speak for myself as well as you. Your blood pressure's up to 250 and my gall bladder is a bag of stones. Make way for the young! May they commit the self-same follies and die of the same diseases.

GENERAL. But I love her, Doctor, and I'm young!

(*Enter the* MAID *up the stairs.*)

MAID. (*Crosses Down Center.*) Will you please say if I am to serve dinner, sir? (DOCTOR *drifts to Up Right window.*) If we wait much longer, the devilled mushrooms won't be devilled mushrooms any more.

GENERAL. Oh shut up about your mushrooms! We'll call them something else then.

MAID. And there's Father Ambrose drinking white wine in the pantry. He says he'll wait as long as you please, sir—(*Crosses Right—lights lamp.*) but what he has to tell you is too important to put off till tomorrow.

GENERAL. Feed *him* the devilled mushrooms. What does he want, today of all days?

MAID. I already suggested he should eat something. (*Crosses Left to Center.*) He won't. He says the excitement of what he has to tell you has quite spoilt his appetite. (DOCTOR—*Up Right, turns to listen.*) But my word he's catching up on the white wine! I don't know if he helps himself like that at Mass but if you don't see him soon, whatever it is he has to tell you is going to be pretty muddled. I think he's going off his head. He says it's providence and we'll have to say some Masses in thanksgiving.

GENERAL. Why, what's Providence been up to this time?

MAID. He says he can tell no one but yourself, sir. It's a secret between Providence and him.

GENERAL. Well, tell them both to wait. (*Exit* MAID *Up Center and down the stairs.*) My reason is tottering, I can feel it. I can't have lost her so stupidly after seventeen years the way one loses a dog in the street. With her lost to me, there's nothing left but a ludicrous old pantaloon, who never saw a single one of his gestures through to its conclusion. (*Rises, crosses Center.*) I have the impression that Lieutenant St. Pé is lying bloodless on a field of battle, not even wounded in the fight—(DOCTOR *"sees"* GHISLAINE *and* GASTON *out window.*) some idiot's rifle blew up in his back a few minutes before zero hour— but that all the same he is going to die. Doctor, if I've lost her— (*Crosses Right to* DOCTOR.)

DOCTOR. (*Who has been looking out of the window.*) No, General, you have not lost her. Here she is, with her ravisher, all rosy from the evening air.

(*The* SECRETARY, *tomato-red, and* GHISLAINE, *her eyes on the ground, enter up the stairs and appear in the doorway.*)

GENERAL. (*Rushing forward in relief, leads* GHISLAINE *Down Center—*GASTON *follows Left of her.*) Ghislaine . . . this unaccountable stroll—I nearly died of fright. (*Sits sofa—she stands Center.*)

GHISLAINE. (*In her usual slightly solemn manner.*) My dear, will you ask the doctor to leave us for a moment? Gaston, leave us too, please. (*Turns to him.*)

SECRETARY. (*Step Down Center. Self-assured though a little sombre.*) Very well. But only for a moment. (*Exits Down Left.*)

GENERAL. Only for a moment? What's got into the young puppy? He never dared speak in that tone to anyone in his life before!

DOCTOR. (*To the* GENERAL *on his way out.*) Courage,

ACT III WALTZ OF THE TOREADORS

Lieutenant! Something tells me this is going to be your last campaign. (DOCTOR *goes out Center and down the stairs.*)

GENERAL. (*Timidly.*) Are you going to explain, Ghislaine?

GHISLAINE. (*Turns to* GENERAL.) Yes my dear, I'll tell you. It's quite simple. I love that young man.

GENERAL. You're joking. And it isn't funny, Ghislaine. Why thundering Hades, two hours ago you'd never even seen the fellow!

GHISLAINE. (*Crosses Down Right to Left end of sofa.*) Had I seen you before the Saumur Ball? And yet the very second when you took me by the waist I fell in love with you. Those seventeen years took nothing away, but added nothing, either, to my love.

GENERAL. That wonderful mad gift of yourself in one moment is something I have always understood and loved you for. But this isn't the same thing at all.

GHISLAINE. (*Transparently.*) Why isn't it, Leon?

GENERAL. Well, because . . . at the Saumur ball—it was me.

GHISLAINE. (*Gently.*) Well?

GENERAL. Well, dammit all, it's not for me to say so, but I was brilliant, I was witty, I was young. And I desired you madly—that counts for something too. But him!

GHISLAINE. (*Crosses Left to Right desk chair.*) He is retiring—or he was—a little naïve perhaps, but you see, my dear—now how can I put it?—For a woman those are opposing qualities, but equally appealing—we love everything. It's like having to choose at a fitting, between a green silk and a pink one. (*Crosses Down a step.*) I might add that he is young, younger even than you were at Saumur, and that he desires me too.

GENERAL. (*Rises spluttering with laughter, crosses Left a step.*) Him? That nonentity? That mooncalf?

GHISLAINE. Leon, I forbid you to insult him!

GENERAL. (*Beside himself, crosses Left and Up to doors.*) Try and stop me! So he desires you, does he?

(*Turns to her a step.*) Do you expect me to believe that, when he saw you, his anaemic blood gave one leap? Don't make me laugh. Say he was speechless—say he knelt at your feet, recited poetry *perhaps*—but don't tell me the boy desires you—it's grotesque!

GHISLAINE. But he proved it, my dear.

GENERAL. How? How could he have proved it to you? Let a real man, worthy of that title, take you in his arms tonight. (*Crosses Left to her.*) And it will be tonight, my dearest, I swear it—let a real man once make love to you, God dammit; and all the rest will disappear like so much smoke.

GHISLAINE. (*Superbly.*) I know. It *is* all so much smoke, my dear. (*Crosses Down Right to Right of sofa.*) Because at long last, someone has made love to me. (*Turns to him.*) I'll shout it to the world, I'm not ashamed. What words do you need then, to make you understand? I belong to him.

GENERAL. (*Step Down Center.*) He dared, that two-faced, vice-ridden little villain?!! That brute? Took you by force, did he? I'll kill him!

GHISLAINE. (*Strongly.*) No, no, my dear, not by force. (*Romantically.*) He took me, and I gave myself, and I am his now, for always.

GENERAL. (*Stricken, crosses Down Right to her, holds out his hands to her, suddenly humble.*) Ghislaine, it's all a nightmare. I'll help you to forget it . . . (*Starts to embrace her.*)

GHISLAINE. (*Drawing away from him.*) No, Leon, you must not touch me any more, only he may touch me now. And you should know how faithful I can be.

GENERAL. (*Sits sofa.*) But when he touched you, you had fallen on your head, you were pumped full of sedative, you didn't even know who was touching you. You thought that it was me!

GHISLAINE. The first few times, yes. But afterwards I knew quite well. He touched me, he really touched me! (*Crosses Right and Up near window.*) And all of a sudden I was no longer sad and lonely and drifting with the

ACT III WALTZ OF THE TOREADORS

tide, I found my footing on the shore at last and I shall never be alone again—at table, at mass, in my wide, wide bed. Don't you see what a wonderful adventure it is? (*Crosses Left to Center.*) You would be a tiny bit glad too if you really loved me, Leon.

GENERAL. I do love you, Ghislaine, but— (*Turns to her.*)

GHISLAINE. Then why not share my joy and let everyone be happy? (*Crying out.*) I am not alone any more! You so often wished it for me. You used to say I should have a companion—

GENERAL. Yes, but a female—

GHISLAINE. I have a male companion now, it's so much better! (*Crosses Up Right—to Right Center window.*) We'll meet from time to time just as we used to do. He said he would permit it. Although between ourselves, my dear, I rather doubt it. He's insanely jealous, do you know that? He says he won't let me out of his sight! Oh! My dear, I'm so happy. I am no longer a dog without a collar. I have a little cord around my neck with my owner's name on it. How good it feels!

GENERAL. (*At Down Right window.*) Lieutenant St. Pé! Don't leave me! What is happening?

GHISLAINE. (*Heedless of the interruption, crossing Left.*) You say he has no wit. Not with men perhaps, not with you, but what does that matter to me? To me he says the prettiest things. He told me that we must swim abreast towards the ideal as if towards a lifebuoy, and that the only proper way to swim is two by two.

GENERAL. (*Rises.*) I might have known it! Did he also tell you that life was one long family lunch with napkin rings, forks of different shapes and sizes and a bell push under the table?

GHISLAINE. What are you suggesting, spiteful? He says poetic things. He says life is but a holiday, a ball . . . (*She twirls.*)

GENERAL. (*With an involuntary cry of pain.*) A ball! (*Sits sofa.*)

GHISLAINE. Yes, isn't that a sweet idea? A ball of a

night, and we must make haste he says, before the lamps go out. I loved him from the very first, I told you so, yet I had got so into the way of thinking love was nothing but one endless vigil, that when he asked me to be his I wanted to cry— Later! Tomorrow! Do you know what he said then? (*Step Right.* GENERAL *shakes his head. Triumphantly.*) He said "At once! At once, my darling!" (*Crosses to above desk.*) Now, who but he would say a thing like that? At once! It's wonderful. I never guessed that one could have something at once!

SECRETARY. (*Enters at Up Center doors, his suspicions aroused but resolved to stand no nonsense.*) The moment is up, Ghislaine. (*Crosses Down Center.*)

GHISLAINE. (*Flustered crosses Up to Left of him.*) Oh, I'm sorry, Gaston.

GENERAL. (*Bearing down on him.*) I'm sorry, Gaston! So there you are, Don Juan! The pretty turtle doves! Just look at them, will you? It's enough to make a cat laugh! What the devil do you take me for, the pair of you? (*Rises and crosses Up Center.*) Death and damnation, I'll show you what I'm made of! (*The* DOCTOR *comes upstairs and appears in the doorway.*) Come in Doctor, come in. You're just in time. Do you know what they've just told me, these two starry-eyed cherubs here? They're in love with each other, if you please. (DOCTOR *drifts Right to above sofa head.*) Yes sir, since two hours ago! And what's more they haven't wasted any time. Some folk have a scruple or two, some folk wait a little while—not they. In the woods, anyhow, like animals. And they expect my blessing into the bargain! God almighty, have they completely lost every scrap of moral sense? (*A step Up Right*—GASTON *and* GHISLAINE *clear to Right end of desk.*)

DOCTOR. (*Has drifted Down Right below chair Center.*) Lieutenant St. Pé. (*Step Left.*)

GENERAL. (*Thundering, crosses Right to him.*) General! Please to address me by my proper rank! (*Crosses Up Center to screen doors, turns front.*) I'll show them who I am! I am going to put on my uniform and all my

ACT III   WALTZ OF THE TOREADORS   65

decorations! No, it'll take too long. Aha, so you seduce young girls, do you, eh? Play cock of the roost, sir, would you? Well, me young jacko, (*Crosses Down to* SECRETARY.) when you've got guts you must show 'em, and otherwise than with the ladies—and that may not prove quite so funny. (*Crosses Down Center.*) Fetch me two swords, someone! Those two up there, on the wall. (*Points, pushes desk to wall, gets Right chair, gets up on desk, lifts chair up, stands on it and starts to unhook swords.*) And no need for seconds, either. The Doctor can stand by with his clobber.

(SECRETARY *crosses Right to Right Center.*)

GHISLAINE. (*Crosses Right to* SECRETARY.) Oh my God he wants blood! He's a cannibal!

DOCTOR. General, you aren't going to start all that again?

GENERAL. And you down there, you hold your tongue too, sir! I haven't forgotten that business of the letters.

GHISLAINE. (*Crosses Left to Down Left of him. Holding his legs.*) Leon! I love him! And if you love me, as you say, you won't hurt him.

GENERAL. The hell I won't! I'll cut off his—(*Pause.*) —ears, Madam. I'll kill him. (*Working on swords.*)

DOCTOR. (*A step Left below sofa.*) General, get down from that chair!

SECRETARY. (*With great nobility to* DOCTOR.) Though I have never held a sword, if the General insists, I am prepared to fight.

GHISLAINE. (*Crosses Right to Left of* SECRETARY.) Gaston, not you! Not you! Let him fight by himself!

DOCTOR. (*Left a step.*) General, it would be murder. He's a child.

GENERAL. (*Still struggling to get the swords down.*) There are no children any more. If he's a child let him go and play with his hoop. Holy suffering bloodstained billicans, who's the double dyed blockhead who put up these swords!!! (*Calling unthinkingly.*) Gaston!

SECRETARY. (*Running up.*) Yes sir?

GENERAL. Give me a hand, my boy.

SECRETARY. (*Keen.*) Yes, sir. (*Crosses to desk, climbs on it and jumps for swords.* GHISLAINE *crosses Right to below Left end of sofa.*)

GENERAL. What the devil are you doing there, sir? Get down! (*He does—crosses Center.*) Doctor, come and help me, will you?

DOCTOR. General, I refuse to be a party any longer to this tragic tomfoolery. You have no right to provoke this lad. (*Sits Down Right chair.*)

GENERAL. (*Groping for sword.*) Did he or did he not consider himself old enough to take the woman I love?

GHISLAINE. But you never would take her at all!

GENERAL. I know my manners. Besides, I was going to. (*Starts to get swords, changes his mind and gets off chair.*) Why what a fool I am! It's so much simpler than that! (*Sits chair leaning Right over back.*) Come to think of it, he *is* a child. How old are you exactly, my boy?

SECRETARY. (*At Center.*) Twenty in strawberry time, sir. The twenty-third of May.

GENERAL. Twenty in strawberry time, splendid. In order to marry then, unless I'm much mistaken, you need your parents' consent, do you not?

SECRETARY. Why recall in her presence the painful circumstances attendant on my birth? I have no parents, sir, as you well know. I am a foundling.

GHISLAINE. Ah!

GENERAL. (*Climbing down from the chair.*) True. But you have a guardian, have you not, a venerable churchman, Father Lambert, I think I'm right in saying? We'll see if Father Lambert will consent to the marriage when I've told him a thing or two. (*Jumps to floor, runs Up Center to hall and shouts down the stairs.*) Eugenie, Eugenie. The curé! The curé, quickly! Send Father Ambrose up at the double. (GHISLAINE *crosses Right a step.*) She's quite right, it *is* Providence that brings the fellow here, for once. (*Turns in hall entrance.*) I'll bet my

ACT III WALTZ OF THE TOREADORS 67

braces Father Lambert will never let you marry an adventuress! (*Crosses Down Right to* GHISLAINE.)

GHISLAINE. Oh Leon! How could you! (*Crosses Right to Down Right window.*)

(*Enter the* PRIEST *up the stairs. Starts Left toward* SECRETARY.)

GENERAL. (*Turns Left.*) Ah, there you are, Father.

FATHER AMBROSE. (*Whirls—crosses Right to* GENERAL *Down Right Center.*) General, at last! (*Shakes hands.*)

GENERAL. You take the words out of my mouth. A matter of the utmost importance.

FATHER AMBROSE. (*Simultaneously.*) A revelation of the utmost interest.

GENERAL. The peace and honor of the family. A watchful firmness.

FATHER AMBROSE. (*Simultaneously.*) The joy and sanctification of the home. A sacred duty. (*They both stop—start again—then.*)

GENERAL. After you.

FATHER AMBROSE. After you. No, on second thoughts, me first. It's too serious. General, may I speak freely before everyone? (*Crosses Up Center a step.*)

GENERAL. (*Sits sofa Right end.*) If you like. But make haste. I'm in a hurry.

FATHER AMBROSE. But we are all friends here, I see—friends who will soon be as deeply moved as I . . .

SECRETARY. If I am in the way, General, I can withdraw.

FATHER AMBROSE. (*Crossing Left to* SECRETARY. *Mysteriously.*) No, my son, you are not in the way. Far from it. (*Turns Center to* GENERAL.) General, it is with deep emotion that I recognize in this the hand of Providence.

GENERAL. No preambles! Come to the point, Father, come to the point. I have to talk to you about this young rascal here.

FATHER AMBROSE. (*Step Right.*) So have I. When I

brought Gaston to you for the post of secretary, I had indeed no inkling . . .

GENERAL. Come to the point, I say. I'm an old soldier. In a couple of words.

FATHER AMBROSE. (*At Center.*) Heaven has nevertheless willed it, in its infinite mansuetude and the exquisite delicacy of its Grace . . .

GENERAL. In a couple of words I say! Not a syllable more or else I'll speak myself.

FATHER AMBROSE. Very well. You have asked for it, General, but it may sound a little crude. Montauban: Lea. (*Crosses Right to Left end of sofa.*)

GENERAL. What do you mean, Montauban: Lea. What's that, an address?

FATHER AMBROSE. (*Laughs.*) You see how difficult it is in a couple of words. (*Steps Left to Center.*) Allow me to amplify a little. There lived in 1890 at Montauban, where the 8th Dragoons were on manoeuvres, a young dressmaker by the name of Lea.

GENERAL. (*Racking his brains.*) Lea? Lea? Holy codfish, Lea! Well, what about her? You don't know what army life can be, your reverence. I could recite you a whole almanack on that account.

FATHER AMBROSE. There was also a dashing captain, dashing but alas—(*Looks at* GENERAL.) very fickle, very careless of a young girl's honour. This captain, the whole while the manoeuvres lasted, gave young Lea to believe he loved her. Perhaps indeed he did.

GENERAL. My dear fellow, why of course! Lea! A ravishing girl, Doctor. A dark-haired filly with eyes a man could drown in—reserved, prudish almost, but in bed of an evening—oh, my dear fellow . . . ! (*He has inadvertently taken the curé's arm. Latter is shocked—backs up.*) I beg your pardon, Father. Have you had news of this young girl, Father?

FATHER AMBROSE. To begin with she was not exactly a young girl, General, by this time; and she has just yielded up the ghost after a very honorable marriage, releasing by her death Father Lambert of a secret.

ACT III   WALTZ OF THE TOREADORS

GENERAL. (*To* DOCTOR.) Fancy. Twenty years ago already.

FATHER AMBROSE. Twenty years. The exact age of this young man here, less nine months.

GENERAL. What?!!

FATHER AMBROSE. A child was born, unbeknownst to you, of this guilty and transient union. (GENERAL *rises*.) A child entrusted to Father Lambert who in turn entrusted him to me. Gaston, kiss your father!

SECRETARY. (*Sobbing with emotion, throws himself into his father's arms.*) Father! My dear old Father! (FATHER AMBROSE *clears to Left near desk*.)

GENERAL. Don't choke me, you great oaf! Just because he tells you I'm your father there's no call to . . . And look at the size of him! (*Pushes him Up Center a step.*)

DOCTOR. (*Rises, crosses Down Right and behind Right chair.*) General, one sows a wild oat, and see, what should spring up but a young tree.

GHISLAINE. (*In rapture.*) Why then everything is quite simple, now! (*Crosses to Left end of sofa.*) You are the man I have loved all along! It's you, Leon, you! Young and free, and even handsomer than your own self! (*Takes both their hands; between them.*) I knew those hands reminded me of something—

GENERAL. Don't overdo it, it's becoming indecent.

GHISLAINE. (*Flying into* SECRETARY's *arms*.) Gaston, we are free to love each other.

SECRETARY. Thank you, Father.

GENERAL. (*Mimicking him.*) That's right, everything is settled. Simple as pie, isn't it? Thank you, Father! Ha, so I'm your father, am I? Right. I refuse to give my consent. (*Turns away Right.*)

GHISLAINE. (*Crosses Right a step above sofa.*) What?

GENERAL. Do not protest, Madam. I do not wish my son to form an alliance with just anybody. I shall make the necessary enquiries.

GHISLAINE. Leon! After all this time that you've known . . .

SECRETARY. (*Clasps hands.*) Father! Dearest Father! It's so good to have a father.

DOCTOR. (*The last.*) Lieutenant St. Pé.

GENERAL. All right. My part in this is growing more and more ridiculous. I give up. (*Sits sofa.*) Death and damnation, let them marry then, and never let me hear any more about anything! (SECRETARY *crosses Up Right, joins* GHISLAINE, *they start Right—stop as the* TWO GIRLS *enter Up the stairs, filthy, dirty, wrapped in blankets and crying.*) Oh Lord, what is it now?

ESTELLE. (*Crosses Down Center.* GHISLAINE *drifts Right to Right of window.*) We really did jump in the lake, Papa, and we swam right out to the middle—

SIDONIA. (*Right of* ESTELLA.) Until we could swim no longer—

GENERAL. What then?

ESTELLA. Then we came back.

GENERAL. Quite right. You can always die some other time. He's your brother, little sillies. So you see there wasn't any need to go and drown yourselves.

THE GIRLS. Our brother?

GENERAL. Yes. I have just heard the news.

SECRETARY. (*Embarrassed.*) That simplifies everything, young ladies. (*A step Left.*) Now I can love you both.

GHISLAINE. (*Jealous.*) Gaston, I forbid you! (*In seventh heaven, to the* DOCTOR.) What a man! Isn't he dreadful?

SIDONIA. Our brother? But Papa, how can that be?

ESTELLE. Why didn't Mother know?

GENERAL. I haven't time to explain. Ask Father Ambrose. He did the trick with the help of Providence. They're going to be married. (GASTON *crosses Right, joins* GHISLAINE, AMBROSE *gestures to shush him.*) He'll explain it all to you one day in Sunday School.

ESTELLE. Papa, if this lady is to be married, won't we need new dresses for the wedding?

GENERAL. (*Acidly.*) Naturally.

ESTELLE. I want to be in duck egg blue.

ACT III   WALTZ OF THE TOREADORS   71

SIDONIA. And I want to be in yellow.

FATHER AMBROSE. (*Crosses Right to Center.*) One moment, my children. I feel that Providence has more than shown today that its bounty extends over us all. The chapel is close by. What do you say to a little prayer, all together, by way of thanksgiving? Won't you join us, General? (*A step Right.*) Once won't make a habit of it. Besides I'm sure that deep down you believe in Providence.

GENERAL. I shall have to, now that it's beginning to take notice of me. But as to saying thank you, really— (*Looks at* SECRETARY *and* GHISLAINE.) today my heart wouldn't be in it. Tomorrow, Father, tomorrow. (*The* PRIEST *shoos the* GIRLS *out Up Center, then goes down the stairs.* SECRETARY *looks at* GHISLAINE, *crosses Left and kisses* GENERAL *on cheek; then crosses Up Center to screen doors to wait for* GHISLAINE. *She goes to* GENERAL *and starts to touch him,* SECRETARY *reaches his arm out to her; she joins him and they exit down the stairs. Looks at hall and back.*) What a farce!

DOCTOR. (*Crosses Up to Right Center window.*) Yes, General. Darkness is falling. We must sound the curfew. (*Crosses Left to above Left of* GENERAL. *Singing a little flat.*) Da da! Da da! Da di di da di di da. . . .

GENERAL. Stop that! What do you take me for? That's the Infantry Lights Out!

DOCTOR. (*Making conversation at Left end of sofa.*) I beg your pardon. Eh—how does it go exactly—in the cavalry?

GENERAL. (*In a cracked voice.*) Da di! Da di! Da . . . I haven't the heart for it. It's too silly. (*Softly.*) Lieutenant St. Pé. I want to live. I want to love. I want to give my heart as well, dear God!

DOCTOR. (*Pats him.*) General, nobody wants it any more. Let it unswell quietly, that old over-tender sponge. You should have sown fewer wild oats and had the courage to hurt while there was still time. Life should be led like a cavalry charge, General. They ought to have told you that at Saumur. My poor old friend, shall I tell you the moral of this story? One must never understand one's enemy or one's wife. One must never understand anyone for that matter, or one will die of it. (*Crosses Left, picks up bag, crosses Up Right Center above* GENERAL.) Heigh-ho, I must go home to Madame Bonfant and her scenes. I think you will do very nicely on your own. (*He pats him on the shoulder.*) See you very soon. (*Shakes hands.*)

GENERAL. (*Motionless.*) Yes, yes.

(*The* DOCTOR *stops in hall, looks back—then exits down stairs.*)

GENERAL'S WIFE. (*Off.*) Leon!
GENERAL. Yes.
GENERAL'S WIFE. Are you there?
GENERAL. Yes. (*Rises.*)
GENERAL'S WIFE. Good. I'm going to have a little nap. Don't do anything in the meantime.

GENERAL. (*He crosses Up Left to set corner—puts hand on gun, shudders and cries suddenly.*) Lieutenant St. Pé. Graduated second from Saumur! Take aim. Steady! Fire! (*Lifts gun in holster. He stands quite still. A shadow appears on the terrace, holding a broom. It is the new* MAID. *She comes upstairs into room on level with* GENERAL.)

MAID. Did you call, sir?
GENERAL. (*Starting.*) Eh? What? No, I didn't call. Who are you?
MAID. I'm the new girl, sir. The new chambermaid you engaged this morning.
GENERAL. (*Looking at her absently, then stroking his moustache.*) Ah yes, of course, by Jove, yes, yes. What was I thinking of? And what is your name, my dear?
MAID. Pamela, sir.
GENERAL. Pamela. Fancy that now. Pamela. And the prettiest bosom in the world too. What is all this nonsense about our having a soul? Do you believe in it? He's a fool, that doctor. Put your broom down, my

child. (*She leaves it against sofa.*) It's a bit late to be sweeping up now. And there is never enough dust on things. We must let it settle. You know, you'll find this an easy sort of place. (*Puts gun back, crosses Right a step to her.*) I'm an old youngster and I don't ask for very much—provided folks are nice to me. You haven't seen my roses, have you? Come, I'll show you round the garden, and if you're a good girl I'll give you one. It doesn't bother you, does it, Pamela, if I put my arm round your waist? (*He does.*)

MAID. (*Simply.*) No sir, but what will Madam say?

GENERAL. Madam will say nothing so long as you don't tell her. (*She puts her arm around him.*) That's a good girl. It's nicer like this, don't you think? Not that it means anything, but still, one feels less lonely, in the dark.

(*They go out, an absurd couple, into the dark garden. "LIGHTS OUT"—the cavalry's this time, is heard in the distance—played by a distant bugle in some barracks in the town.*)

THE CURTAIN FALLS

PROPERTY LIST

THE WALTZ OF THE TOREADORS

Set Props—Main Room—(Hanging)

4 lace curtains—on 2 windows Right stage
4 curtain rods
1 mattress—outside Right Center window
2 green sheets—1 covering mattress—1 spare padding—under mattress
4 hanging vines—outside windows
3 trunk vines—outside windows
1 large oil painting—hanging on backing behind double-doors
1 flag holder—Left of double doors
5 flags—in holder
1 antelope hat rack—hanging Right of scrim and one half way up
1 holster and strap with revolver—hanging from antelope—holster level with bottom of scrim
1 large scrim and bamboo frame—Up Left Center
1 canteen and strap—hanging from bottom of scrim
1 binoculars and case with strap—hanging from bottom of scrim
3 dowels with horn decorations—hanging from upper corners and Left Center of scrim frame
2 bright red drapes—from dowels—over scrim
1 long striped drape—from dowels and frame—over scrim
2 spears—over drapes—crossed
1 red shield-shape sword holder—over center of scrim—4 removable buttons
2 swords—crossed—on sword holder
1 polo stick—hanging Left scrim frame

PROPERTY PLOT

1 8 foot bookcase—Up Left corner
1 man on horse back statuette—top of bookcase
1 Roman helmet
1 engraved scabbard and belt with sabre—between bookcase and door of morning room Down Left
2 powder horns
1 red velvet pad
1 round removable backboard—over morning room door
10 swords—on back board
2 daggers—on back board
1 equestrian picture—black frame—Right of morning room door
1 equestrian picture—gold frame—under black frame picture
1 ground-cloth
2 4 x 20 tabe off 6 x 18 wings
1 4 x 10 red tapestry—from top masking flat in morning room

Furniture

1 armchair—Down Right
1 marble-top table—Down Right above armchair
1 chaise longue—Right Center—4 rubber casters
1 storage bench—Center of window Up Right Center
1 round stool—carpet covered—front of bench (Act One only)
1 moorish coffee table Up Right corner between middle window and double doors
1 desk—Down Left Center
1 moroccan chair—above desk
2 secretary chairs—either side of desk
1 wastebasket —plays of rear Right leg of desk—Act One only
1 Moorish map stand (inlaid designs) Right of morning room door—secured to flat
1 globe on map stand
1 lamp with removable chimney and glove on marbletop table

PROPERTY PLOT

1 large blue bowl on Moorish coffee table
1 potted palm in green bucket in blue bowl

Small Props:
1 purple table cover—on marble top table
1 china ash tray with matches—top table
1 small yellow book—top table
Candle—in lamp
1 business size blotter and holder—on desk
1 small blotter—on desk
Stationery—on desk
Glass paper weight—on desk
2 pens—on desk
1 tobacco box—on desk
1 pipe—on desk
2 large books—Left side of desk
Cardboard portfolio—Left side of desk
2 small books—on desk
Cheroots in tin—on desk
3 framed photos—on desk
Demitasse cup and saucer with coffee—on desk
Brass coffee pot—on desk
Blank manuscript—in desk drawer
Envelope—in desk drawer
Ink bottle—on desk
Fez—on globe
Pencils
1 china box and tray (flowered) on cabinet
Assorted bottles—on cabinet
1 labelled bottle and cork with water—inside cabinet
Assorted bottles—inside cabinet
Assorted bottles—inside cabinet, left shelves

BEDROOM

Hanging Props
1 scalloped border—overhead
Two-fold black portal Left
Single portal Right
14 x 8 back tab Up Left

PROPERTY PLOT

6 x 20 border over and behind bedroom
6 x 24 overhead border
1 traveling masking curtain with pulley—behind scrim
Wall to wall carpeting—on kidney shaped platform
2 lace drapes with pull-backs—window
Blue lined canopy—over bed
Pleated print bed drape around bed
1 rectangular picture—on wall Right of bed
1 round picture
1 rectangular picture—over escape door
2 rectangular pictures—on escape door
2 rectangular pictures—on wall Left of door
1 hanging mirror—over cabinet
9 snapshots and cards—stuck in mirror

Furniture

2 chairs—1 against Right wall—I Left Center
1 bed—against wall Center
1 two-step with carpeting—against bed—Right side
1 covered foot stool—against bed—Left side
1 night table—head of bed—Left side
1 lamp with globe—on night table
1 cabinet—down Left
1 bolster—on bed

Small Props

Mattress—on bed
2 pillows with lace covers—on bed
Padding—under mattress—strike after first scene
1 muslin sheet—on bed
1 muslin sheet with lace—top sheet on bed
1 muslin sheet—covering bolster
1 quilt—on bed
1 water carafe and glass with fresh water—on night table
1 handkerchief—on night table
1 pill bottle and top—on night table
1 cologne bottle with water—on night table
5 standing pictures with frames—on cabinet
1 standing picture—no frame—on cabinet against wall

1 china cologne bottle with top on cabinet
1 china coffee pot and burner (white) on cabinet

Off-stage Props

Doctor's bag (Doctor—11)
1 reticule (St. Euverte—11)
1 small revolver (pearl handled) 11
Note pad (Secretary—11)
Pencil (Secretary—11)
Coffee cup and saucer with coffee (Maid—12)
Wine bucket—set under marbletop table—21)
Napkin—in bucket
Bottle with wine—in bucket
Corkscrew—set on marbletop 21
2 wine glasses on marbletop
1 broom (Pamela—31)
Jewelry wrapped in tissue paper—**on marble top 31**
1 pink letter—on marbletop 31
1 blue letter—set on bed 12

THE WALTZ OF THE TOREADORS

COSTUMES

GENERAL ST. PÉ: 2 piece blue-wool uniform with a single inch-and-a-half red stripe down each trouser leg. Gold braid on either side of the high collar. Black silk braid with silver stars on each lower sleeve. Black ankle boots.

HIS WIFE: White-wool skirt trimmed with Irish lace valences. Chiffon bodice with white lace over it. Sleeves of chiffon with white lace over it. White knitted ankle-length booties.

ESTELLE: Act One, Scene 1 (first entrance): Green-silk dress trimmed with collar and cuffs of lace. Black high-laced shoes. White stockings. Gaiters. Same Scene (second entrance): Short white embroidered dress. Same shoes, hose, gaiters. Act Two, Scene 1: Long white embroidered dress. Same shoes, hose, gaiters. Act Three: Grey blanket spotted with mud. Bare feet.

SIDONIA: Act One, Scene 1 (first entrance): Blue-silk dress trimmed with collar and cuffs. Black high-laced shoes. White stockings. Same Scene (second entrance): Short white embroidered dress. Same shoes, hose, gaiters. Act Two, Scene 1: Long white embroidered dress. Same shoes, hose, gaiters. Act Three: Grey blanket spotted with mud. Bare feet.

GASTON: Black-wool suit with 4 button jacket. White shirt. Black and white four-in-hand tie. Black button shoes. Black stockings.

GHISLAINE: Rose chiffon dress over pink net and satin. Deep rose satin belt with sash in rear. Pink satin slippers with baby louis heels. White silk hose tinted pink. Light tan long velvet coat, tan beige hat with white silk veil, and beige gloves are worn during Act One, Scene 1. Hat is discarded before first entrance in Act One, Scene 2. Coat is discarded before the second entrance of Act One, Scene 2.

MME. DUPONT-FREDAINE: Purple faille skirt. Top of purple taffeta with velvet stripes. Velvet collar with ruchings of white on sleeves and cuffs. Vestee of lace. Red felt hat with red velvet trim and gold brocaded band. Purple gloves. Grey suede strap slippers with baby louis heels. Black silk hose.

DOCTOR BONFANT: Grey and black striped morning suit. Tan vest. White shirt. Grey and black striped cravat. Tie pin. Black shoes with grey spats.

FATHER AMBROSE: Black trousers beneath. Heavy wool cassock. Black belt with sash. Black work shoes. Black hose. Small lens steel rimmed glasses.

FIRST MAID: Grey and black striped cotton dress with long sleeves. Tight bodice. White collar and cuffs. White scalloped apron with bib. White House-maids' cap. White petticoat. Black buttoned shoes.

NEW MAID. Grey and black striped cotton dress with long sleeves. Tight bodice. Blue and white apron with short bib in front. White petticoat. Black laced shoes.